"Now, then, this morning someone was saying how the Lancers were going to be pushovers, right?" Coach Allen said.

"Well, they are smaller," he continued. "But their score looks pretty tall to me right now."

"They're better than we are, Coach," Damont said.

"Could be," Coach Allen said. "And their coach could be better than I am, too. But let's not look at it that way, because if we do, we beat ourselves." He held up one finger. "You know, I thought we were going into this game with a major disadvantage. Can anyone guess what it is?"

Wishbone jumped up. "I know! I know! Call on the dog!"

Joe said, "Overconfidence, sir?"

"Overconfidence," Coach Allen agreed.

Wishbone sat down. "I was going to say that."

Books in The Adventures of **wishbone**™ series:

Be a Wolf!
Salty Dog
The Prince and the Pooch
Robinhound Crusoe
Hunchdog of Notre Dame
Digging Up the Past
The Mutt in the Iron Muzzle
Muttketeer!
A Tale of Two Sitters
Moby Dog
The Pawloined Paper
Dog Overboard!
Homer Sweet Homer
Dr. Jekyll and Mr. Dog
A Pup in King Arthur's Court
The Last of the Breed
Digging to the Center of the Earth
Gullifur's Travels
*Terrier of the Lost Mines**

Books in The Super Adventures of **wishbone**™ series:

Wishbone's Dog Days of the West
The Legend of Sleepy Hollow
Unleashed in Space
*Tails of Terror**

*coming soon

The Adventures of WISHBONE™

GULLIFUR'S TRAVELS

by Brad Strickland and Barbara Strickland

Inspired by *Gulliver's Travels*
by Jonathan Swift
WISHBONE™ created by Rick Duffield

Big Red Chair Books™, *A Division of **Lyrick Publishing**™*

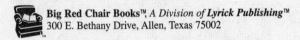 **Big Red Chair Books**™, *A Division of **Lyrick Publishing***™
300 E. Bethany Drive, Allen, Texas 75002

©1999 Big Feats Entertainment, L.P.

Edited by Kevin Ryan

Copy edited by Jonathon Brodman

Continuity editing by Grace Gantt

Cover concept and design by Lyle Miller

Interior illustrations by Jane McCreary

Wishbone photograph by Carol Kaelson

Library of Congress Catalog Card Number: 98-88462

ISBN: 1-57064-403-9

First printing: July 1999

10 9 8 7 6 5 4 3 2 1

To our nieces and nephew—
Emily, Ian, and Sarah

FROM THE BIG RED CHAIR . . .

Oh . . . hi! Wishbone here. You caught me right in the middle of some of my favorite things—books. Let me welcome you to THE ADVENTURES OF WISHBONE. In each of these books, I have adventures with my friends in Oakdale and imagine myself as a character in one of the greatest stories of all time. This story takes place in the spring, when Joe is twelve and he and his friends are in the sixth grade—during the first season of my television show.

In *GULLIFUR'S TRAVELS*, I imagine I'm a young doctor named Lemuel Gulliver, from Jonathan Swift's adventure story, *GULLIVER'S TRAVELS*. It's a funny tale about being shipwrecked on strange, faraway islands. It's where giants and tiny people rule, ridiculous ideas make sense, and the person who can make the scariest face lands the best job!

You're in for a real treat, so pull up a chair, grab a snack, and sink your teeth into *GULLIFUR'S TRAVELS!*

Chapter One

Wishbone ran up and down the sidelines of the basketball court. He was just in front of the bleachers, his eyes following every move Joe made. Twelve-year-old Joe wore the red-and-white uniform of the Oakdale Basketball Camp Raiders. The team had been organized for a special week-long Spring Break camp.

Coach Allen clapped his hands and he yelled, "Hustle, Joe, hustle!"

Joe ran across the court, dribbling and dodging defenders. Wishbone winced at the screeching sound of basketball shoes rubbing on the hardwood floor. But even that high-pitched noise did not dampen his enthusiasm. He leaped up. "Shoot, Joe, shoot!"

But Joe had other ideas. Facing a defending player, he made a tight turn. He passed the ball to Lewis Friedman, the smallest player on the Raiders team. Lewis dodged and faked out the player who was covering him. Then Lewis made a perfect shot. The ball sailed through the net without even touching the rim.

Wishbone leaped up onto the bleachers in excitement. "Two points! Way to pass the ball, Joe! Great shot, Lewis!"

As if Coach Allen were listening to the dog, he clapped his hands. "That's great teamwork!" he said. "Good move, Joe. And Lewis, your shooting is getting better all the time!"

"Thanks," Joe said, trying to catch his breath.

Lewis grinned and nodded. "Not bad for only two days' practice and two games," he said.

"But they've been two *hard* days, and two *well-played* games," Coach Allen said with a chuckle. "That's what it takes, boys. Hard practice and hard playing. This is Tuesday, only the second day of practice, and I'm really impressed with the two of you."

The Raiders team had been divided into two sides for the practice session. Damont Jones had been playing defense opposite Joe's group. Damont said, "We could have held 'em if our side knew what they were doing."

Coach Allen shook his head. "I don't know. Joe's side has speed, and the players work well together. I think your side's problem, Damont, is not that you don't know what to do. You just don't work together. Teamwork, remember?"

"That only counts if you have a team worth working with," Damont said.

Wishbone sighed. Why did Damont have to be so sour? Wishbone didn't feel that way. He'd been the unofficial mascot for the Raiders for only two days, but he really felt as if he belonged! He thought, *Why, without my cheering them on, the Raiders wouldn't be half as good as they are. I just wish Damont would join in for once, instead of complaining.*

What was that saying Wishbone had heard? "You can't teach an old dog new tricks?" He thought that was nonsense. With the right kind of tasty treats, you could teach a dog of any age as many tricks as you wanted to. The hard thing, he believed, was to teach Damont to loosen up, have fun, and play as a part of the team. Wishbone, for example, was loving every minute!

Of course, Wishbone got excited about a lot of things. For instance, he could hardly control his enthusiasm at breakfast, mid-morning snack time, lunch, afternoon snack time, dinner, before-bed snack time, and midnight-snack time. Running in Jackson Park with his best friend, Joe Talbot, was a lot of fun, too. But, he thought, for pure noise and great physical activity, nothing could compare with a gym full of basketball players!

It was almost time for lunch. Wishbone trotted over to the other side of the court. There, Coach Allen had the boys sitting down on the bleachers. He was giving them pointers, and everyone was catching his breath. Wishbone's nose twitched. Some of those basketball sneakers were getting pretty smelly. Not to mention the mild burned-rubber aroma they got when their owners screeched to a sudden stop or made a quick change of direction! Wishbone found almost any smell interesting—but at the moment he was most interested in sniffing out a treat. Or, even better, sniffing out lunch!

"Now, we're going to be in our first playoff game

tonight," Coach Allen reminded them. "That's up in Littleton, with the basketball camp from the middle school there. You'll all need to be here at five-fifteen to catch the bus. We pull out at five-thirty."

Wishbone came over and sat at Joe's feet. He looked up as Joe ruffled his ears. "Joe, you're doing fantastic! I just know that with my tips on speed and Coach Allen's advice on shooting, you're going to be a basketball star!"

"Coach Allen," Joe asked, still scratching Wishbone's ears, "is it all right if Wishbone comes to watch us play tonight?"

"Oh, please, come on!" Damont complained from behind Joe. "The last thing that we need is a dog getting car-sick on the bus!"

Wishbone sniffed. "I'll have you know that I *never* get car-sick! I am a well-traveled dog!"

"Well," Coach Allen said, "I'd really like to have our mascot come along. I don't know how the bus driver will feel about having an extra passenger, though. There are insurance rules, I'm sure."

"My mom can drive him over," Joe said.

"In that case, I think Wishbone deserves a court-side seat," the coach replied with a laugh. "Sure, bring him. I'll call over to Littleton and tell Coach Gonzalez to expect him."

"Gonzalez?" Damont asked. "We're gonna be playing the Lancers? Easy win!"

"Bad thinking, Damont," Coach Allen said, shaking his head. "Never underestimate the other team. That's a serious mistake."

Damont said, "But I heard that the Lancers are all

really short! I mean, they're shrimps! In basketball, the tall guys always have the advantage."

Coach Allen pointed a finger to his head. "The *thinking* guys have the advantage," he corrected. "Now, I know Coach Gonzalez. In fact, I played against him quite a few times when we were both in the NBA. I can tell you right now that he's a thinking player *and* a thinking coach. We're going to have to be on our toes tonight."

The coach checked his watch.

"Lunch break," he said. "After lunch, we'll watch some tapes of professional games and I'll point out a few things you might learn from the pros. Then we'll finish up about two-thirty. I'd like for each of you to have a couple of hours' rest before we start off for the game at five-thirty. Now, hit the showers!"

Wishbone couldn't follow Joe into the showers, so he went outside and waited. The basketball camp was being held in the gym at Oakdale College. Wishbone enjoyed the campus. It was green with new spring grass. Crowds of college students walked by. Many enjoyed stopping to pet the handsome white-with-brown-and-black-spots Jack Russell terrier. The dog's only regret was that more college students didn't carry snacks in case they met such a good-looking and very deserving dog.

Joe and the other boys came outside a few minutes later. They carried their lunch in brown-paper bags. The boys walked over to some concrete picnic tables to eat. Joe put a paper plate on the ground. He had brought Wishbone's lunch along with him that morning. Wishbone licked his chops as he watched Joe take out a plastic bag of kibble and empty it into the paper plate. "Now, don't eat the plate," Joe warned.

"No problemo, Joe! But the faster I finish off the kibble, the sooner I can ask for any leftover sandwich crusts!" Wishbone dug in, crunching happily.

"Well?" Lewis asked Joe, as Wishbone ate. "What do you think? I hear that the players on Coach Gonzalez's team *are* kinda short."

Joe shrugged. "Maybe that's true, but I think Coach Allen is right. Height isn't everything."

"Yeah," Damont said in a sour tone. "Lewis should know that. I mean, he's the shortest guy on the Raiders."

"Come on, Damont," Joe said. "Lewis is as good a player as any of us."

"Look," Damont said. "If one team can get a foot closer to the basket than the other team, then the first team's going to win, okay?"

Lewis said, "This time I agree with Damont. I think we're starting out with an easy win."

Sean McMurdo, a friend of Joe's who had a terrific layup shot, said, "I'm with Damont. Let's face it—we tall guys have the edge on the court." Sean was the tallest guy playing for the Raiders, and his long arms gave him an extra advantage at the net.

Wishbone polished off the last of his dry dog food. "Hey, hey, hey! Let's not get . . . uh, size-ist here, okay? I mean, there are some people who even call *me* a little dog, but they— Uh . . . ham. Uh . . . are you going to finish that sandwich, Sean? Do you want your crusts? Huh?"

Sean smiled at Wishbone. "Here you go, fella," he said. The boy tossed the crust of his sandwich—with some very tasty ham left inside—to Wishbone. "Look at him!"

Wishbone leaped from a standing position as high as the tabletop to catch the crust. He snapped his head sideways and chomped on it in one lightning-quick move.

"Way to go, Wishbone!" Lewis said, laughing. "Great passing game you've got there!"

"And Wishbone's not so tall," Joe said with a grin.

Wishbone was wolfing down the treat. "My point exactly, Joe! Except that *I* happen to be just the right size, of course. Mmm, that was good!" He sniffed. "Oh, boy! Someone here has a roast beef sandwich! Scrumptious, nutritious, tasty roast— Oh, it's Damont. Forget I even mentioned it."

Damont never gave Wishbone any treat. He finished off the last bite of his sandwich and muttered, "The way I see it, Coach Allen's gonna use tonight's game to let everybody get out on the court. Then later in the playoffs, when we play a real team—I hear that the Jefferson Giants are supposed to be the toughest—the coach'll know which of us can cut it and which of us come up a little, should I say, short? Huh, Lewis?"

"Knock it off, Damont," Lewis said. He held up half a bologna sandwich. "Hey, Wishbone, want to go for a long one?" He made a couple of tossing motions.

Wishbone ran a short distance away. "Go for it!"

Lewis tossed the half-sandwich so it spun through the air, flying high.

Damont said, "He'll *never* catch that."

Wishbone was already running for it. "Watch me! Steady, get ready . . . *woo-cha!*" The terrier leaped and spun at the same time, positioning himself perfectly for the catch. He snapped his mouth shut on the sandwich, landed, and gave Damont a look. "How would you describe *never,* Damont?"

"Lucky catch," Damont said quickly.

"Nope," Joe replied. "Pure talent."

Later, Wishbone dozed in a darkened classroom as Coach Allen showed his players tapes of professional basketball games on a large-screen television. Sometimes he would rewind the tape to draw their attention to important plays. Once Wishbone looked up when Coach Allen said, "Now watch this guy. Anyone recognize him?"

"It's Reggie Heard," Joe said at once. "My dad coached him!"

"And he's not exactly the tallest man in this game," the coach said. "But watch the fantastic series of shots he makes."

Wishbone blinked at the screen. In fast succession,

the player made one, two, three, four, five, six baskets, all of them with great speed and style. "Whoa! He's terrific! I'd better study this tape. I might pick up some tips on jumping for balls!"

"He scored forty-two points in this game alone," Coach Allen said. "Reggie knows how to make his height *and* his brain work to his advantage. That's something you'll all have to learn, too."

At two-thirty, the players left the gym. Wishbone and Joe headed home. Joe went inside and rested in his room upstairs. Wishbone patrolled the yard to make sure no one would sneak into the yard next door. It belonged to Wanda Gilmore—at least it did legally. But Wishbone considered Wanda's yard his own bone-burying territory. Sometimes a passing dog would discover his buried treasures. Reassured that there was nothing to worry about, he took a long nap in the warm sunshine. He woke up when Ellen drove her station wagon into the driveway. Wishbone jumped up then, fully alert, hoping for a treat.

Ellen Talbot, Joe's lively, brown-haired mom, got out. Wishbone ran to greet her. He admired her intelligence, her cheerfulness, and her cooking—especially her cooking! Ellen smiled at the dog and said, "Hi, Wishbone! I've got something special for you."

Wishbone's tail wagged wildly. "Thank you, Ellen! Thank you, thank you! A thousand times thank you! Uh . . . it's not a new leash, is it?"

Ellen took a couple of bags out of the car, and Wishbone followed her inside. From one of the bags she took a rawhide chew toy shaped like a bone.

Wishbone's mouth watered. "Yum! As usual,

Ellen, your taste in gifts is perfect! Thank you, thank you! A thousand— Oh, right. I already said that. Well, I meant every word!"

As Wishbone gnawed happily on his new chew toy, he heard Joe coming downstairs. "Hi, Mom. I have a game tonight," he said.

"I know, Joe," Ellen replied. "Wanda and I are going to drive over to see it."

"Can Wishbone ride along with you?" Joe asked. He went on to explain that the coach said it would be all right for Wishbone to attend as the team's mascot.

"Sure," Ellen said. "As long as he behaves."

Wishbone looked up with the rawhide bone in his mouth. "Me? Behafe? I always behafe! Good as gold, that'f me!"

"Damont says it's going to be a pretty boring game," Joe said, helping his mom put canned goods in the kitchen cabinets. "We heard that the Littleton Lancers are a short team. Nobody thinks they have a chance of winning."

"Is that what the coach said?" Ellen asked, sounding surprised.

Joe shook his head. "You know coaches. They have to make every game sound like a challenge. But if the Lancers are really as small as everyone says, we ought to rack up a pretty good score."

Wishbone took his rawhide chew toy to the study and hopped into his big red chair. He munched thoughtfully for a while. *I think Joe's catching the "they're small so they must be a bad team" disease. Well, vertically challenged dogs know that's not true. Tall or small—that doesn't matter. What really counts is what's inside the package.*

16

He stopped chewing. *Tall and small . . . that reminds me of a story. A story about a man who learned what it was like to be both the tallest guy around and the smallest. It's a great book, and it says a lot about big people and small people. Its title is* Gulliver's Travels.

Chapter Two

*G*ulliver's Travels was published in 1726. It's the most famous book ever written by author Jonathan Swift. He was an Englishman who lived in Ireland for most of his life. Jonathan Swift made fun of a lot of bad human habits in his book: greed and false pride, foolishness and bad temper. He was a satirist—which meant that as a writer, he liked to let the air out of windbags, laugh at people's weak points when they could not laugh at themselves, and poke fun at foolish ideas that people believed in but never thought much about.

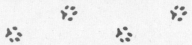

As Wishbone lay in his big red chair, he began to imagine that he was Lemuel Gulliver, the hero of *Gulliver's Travels*. He fantasized that he was a young doctor in England in the year 1699. Wishbone remembered how, in Jonathan Swift's book, Gulliver had told his own story. . . .

My father was a farmer in Nottinghamshire, in the north of England. He was far from rich, but he was able to send me to medical school. However, soon the money ran out. Then I became an apprentice—a student—to a London surgeon, Mr. James Bates. He advised me to study other subjects as well as medicine. I enjoyed mathematics, so I studied navigation and other useful arts. I read as many books as I could get my paws on.

When at last I became a doctor myself, I thought all my money problems had ended. I met, fell in love with, and married Mary Burton. We rented a house, and I set up an office there. Sadly, I soon learned that people didn't trust a very young, inexperienced doctor. Each day I would wake up, tail wagging, thinking, *Today's the day I will make some money!* But each day I was disappointed. I had almost no patients, and soon my wife and I began to fall into debt. I wrote to my old friend, Mr. Bates, for advice. He told me that I could easily get a job as a ship's doctor. Mary and I thought the idea over, and we finally agreed that I would have to try that.

Mr. Bates introduced me to Captain William Pritchard. He was about to sail for the South Seas in his ship, the *Antelope*. It would be a long journey, lasting more than a year, but the pay would be good. So I signed on as the ship's doctor. Then, on May 4, 1699, we sailed from the English port of Bristol.

The voyage was difficult, but we did a good

business in trading many products with the locals. I treated the injuries and the illnesses of the sailors. They soon began to like and respect me a great deal. I started to think that this sailing life was the very thing to make me happy.

And then we hit the rock.

On the fifth of November, 1699, I was in my sickbay, the ship's small hospital. I was mixing some medicines, when I felt the ship jolt so violently that I had to brace all four feet to keep from falling. Dropping the medicine bottle, I ran up on deck immediately, yelling, "What's wrong?"

Captain Pritchard was standing at the front of the ship. He turned, his face pale, and said, "We've struck a hidden rock! The ship has split, and we're sinking. Lower the lifeboats!"

A huge wave hit us from behind. I heard the masts creaking and jumped out of the way just as the mainmast crashed to the deck! The ship began to tilt, until standing on the deck was like standing on the side of a steep roof! Sailors yelled in panic and strained to get the lifeboats over the side and clear of the ship. I realized that I had only a few seconds to get ready to abandon ship.

Quickly I went belowdecks and grabbed a few medical items and some personal belongings. I put them into a waterproof leather pouch and then slung it around my neck. I ran back up on deck to find the ship settling low in the water. Another wave crashed into us! I saw one empty lifeboat still tied to the main ship and dashed over to it. "Men!" I shouted. "Help me launch this boat! Quickly!"

"I'll help, Doctor!" shouted Mr. Hawes, the third mate. "Get over here, some of you! Quickly!"

Mr. Hawes and five other sailors struggled to push the boat over the rail. The deck was tilting even more now! I was scrambling just to keep from falling into the sea. "Give the lifeboat one more hard shove!" I yelled.

With a grunt, Hawes pushed as hard as he could. The boat finally went over the rail and splashed into the sea. "The ship's sinking!" Hawes yelled, as the next great wave hit us.

"Over the side!" I ordered. The sailors all jumped. I leaped up from the deck to the rail and felt the ship tilting dangerously backward. Making a mighty leap, I scrambled into the lifeboat just as the ship sank beneath the waves.

For a while I thought we were safe. Unfortunately, the day was windy, and dark clouds blew up from the north. Before we knew it, a furious storm hit us with gusting winds and endless rain. Soon we lost sight of the other lifeboats.

"Have courage, men!" I shouted. But at that moment, a fierce blast of wind flipped our small boat over and tossed it through the air! I fell into the water, sank a few feet, and kicked my way back to the surface. In all the foam and rain, I could not see the boat, or any of the men.

After half an hour of hard swimming, I realized the storm was passing. When the water grew calm, I tried to look around. My heart sank when I realized I was the only living soul on that wide ocean. All the others must have drowned.

I might have given up, but a wave lifted me high enough to give my sensitive nose a slight, welcome scent of land. I began to swim toward it in a steady dog-paddle. It was my only chance, small though it seemed. I grew so tired that at times I almost sank, but the water splashing into my face always revived me. Finally, after what must have been hours, I felt my front paws touch bottom. I hardly had enough strength left in me to crawl through the breaking waves and trot up onto the sandy shore. I saw very short grass ahead, and I dragged myself to it, then collapsed. It was late afternoon by then. Worn out, I fell into a deep, deep sleep.

I slept for what must have been hours on that soft, comfortable grass. Then I awoke with a start, the morning sun hot on my nose. I felt dry and uncomfortably warm. The sun shone in my eyes. In fact, my mouth was open and I was panting. Groaning, I tried to stand up.

I couldn't. I was flat on my belly and tied down— not with one rope, but with hundreds of threads, or so it seemed. I tugged. Then I felt something on my back. Whatever it was moved! It seemed to be walking right over the top of my head, between my ears, then down onto my nose. I tried to focus my eyes and saw— No, it couldn't be. But it was!

A tiny human creature, maybe one-fifth my size! I quickly calculated that this creature stood about three inches or so in height! He stood on my muzzle! He was

carrying a bow and arrow, and he was aiming the miniature arrow right between my eyes!

"Don't shoot!" I yelled, startling the little man so much that he fell right off!

He scrambled up to his feet again and shouted, *"Hekinah degul!"* Other voices joined in the shouting. I realized that hundreds of the little people were all around me. Alarmed and confused, I jumped to my feet, pulling loose many of the little threads. Tiny figures swung from some of them, desperately trying to hold on!

At the same time, someone yelled, *"Tolgo phonac!"* I whirled around in time to see a whole army of a hundred or so tiny men, armed with bows and arrows. They shot their arrows, and a dozen or more of them hit me on the nose and muzzle, stinging like needles. *"Tolgo phonac!"* ordered the man again. Then another group shot still more arrows at me as I raised my paw to shield my eyes.

"No!" I shouted as more arrows stung my left paw. "No *tolgo phonac! Tolgo phonac* bad! Don't *tolgo* any more *phonacs*, please!" I lay down quickly to show them I meant no harm.

To my surprise, two of the small creatures, a man and a woman, came close to me. The man reached out and pulled an arrow from my paw. The woman used a tiny mop to put some kind of medicine on the wound. It took away the pain. The man made some hand motions, which I assumed meant he was asking whether he should take out more of the arrows. I nodded "yes." I lay still while the two of them crept around, removing all the tiny arrows and treating my wounds. Soon I began to feel much better.

All the while, I felt a terrible hunger and thirst. When the doctors—I thought they were doctors, anyway—had finished removing the arrows, I tried to show by physical movements that I needed food and water. They seemed to understand me, because soon four horses pulled a wagon in front of me. It was loaded down with what smelled like hams and beef roasts—except they were only the size of an acorn! I gulped them down gratefully while all the little people said "Ooh!" and "Ah!" to each mouthful I took. Then another wagon came up, loaded with wooden barrels. Two men took off the tops of these, and I saw that the barrels contained water. I drank it greedily. I suppose all together the barrels held about a pint of liquid. What continued to surprise me was the size of everything around me. From people to food, it was all *very* small!

Then a richly dressed man came to me and gave a long speech. I didn't understand a single word of what he said. At the end, he signaled with his hands. The army came over to me and untied the rest of the thread-ropes, the ones I had not pulled loose. The man signaled for me to wait, and at once I sat down obediently.

Next, swarms of the little people went into the woods nearby. I noticed for the first time that the trees there looked much like our trees back home in England. However, they were all much smaller, the tallest of them not more than three feet high. With a loud noise of sawing and hammering, the workmen cut down the trees, sawed them into planks, and built

25

a huge—for them—wagon. I was amazed at how fast they worked.

By mid-afternoon, the wagon was finished. The man who had made the speech motioned to me that I should climb aboard the wagon, and I did. It groaned as I got my four paws aboard, and it held all my weight. They tied me down so I wouldn't fall off. Then the people hitched dozens of horses to the wagon.

The horses pulled me along the grassy hill, then down and onto a narrow dirt road. Crowds of people followed, pointing at me and shouting. I was amazed and puzzled, all at the same time. I almost thought I was dreaming, but the sun was hot enough, and the wounds from the little arrows still stung a little. Ahead of me I saw a strange sight, a miniature town. We came closer and closer. Then I

realized that, to the people of this country, the toy houses and buildings were real. They actually lived in all of them.

A wall surrounded the tiny town, and the horses dragged my wagon through the widest, highest gate. We went down the main street, though it was a very tight squeeze. I kept my paws and tail tucked in so that I wouldn't accidentally knock over a building!

We came to a tall building with steep roofs and many towers. It was a palace. Trumpeters blew a high-pitched announcement of my arrival from a dozen miniature musical instruments, and a balcony door on the third floor of the building opened. A man and woman stepped out. Both of them wore tiny golden crowns that gleamed in the sunlight. I was untied from the wagon. I sat up. Since they were on the third floor of their palace, they looked at me eye to eye.

Then the man began to make a speech. He waved his arms and pointed at me now and then. He kept using the words *Quinbus Flestrin* when he pointed. I began to understand that it was some kind of name he was giving me, something like "handsome giant," probably.

When he had finished, I lifted a paw and pointed at myself. *"Quinbus Flestrin,"* I said. I heard all the people say "Ooh!" and "Ah!" again. Then I said, *"Quinbus Flestrin*—Lemuel Gulliver."

I lay down on my stomach to show that I meant no harm to anyone. The ruler—by now I was sure the little man was a king or duke, surely someone of royalty—nodded and gave some orders. The men guiding the horses made them move, and they hauled me around to the rear of the palace.

There the man who had first made the long speech to me came toward me alone. He motioned for me to get out of the wagon, which I did, very carefully. Then he pointed for me to follow him.

Some soldiers opened a gate in a high wall—though it was one I could easily have jumped over—and I lowered my body and belly-crawled through, still following the little man.

We entered a courtyard. In the center of it was a marble building about eighteen inches tall. I later learned that it was a temple no longer used. Years earlier, two men had fought inside it, and one had killed the other. The people of that land believed that such an act made the temple unusable, so it had stood empty for generations. My guide opened the doors and showed me I could go inside.

I squeezed in, then saw that it was actually big enough for me to stand in, with plenty of room to stretch out. The little man then indicated to me that he was going to leave, but I had to stay.

"Quinbus Flestrin?" I asked.

The man pointed at me and said, *"Quinbus Flestrin."*

"What *is Quinbus Flestrin?"* I asked him.

I think he understood my tone as a question. Anyway, he went out into the courtyard and picked up a stick. He sketched something in the dirt. I stepped into the courtyard. Leaning close to watch him, I puzzled over it. At first it was just a kind of rough triangle. Then I realized he had drawn a mountain. And it looked a bit like me.

"Living mountain?" I asked. "Is that what *Quinbus Flestrin* means?"

"*Quinbus Flestrin,*" the man repeated after me, and he pointed from the drawing to me. Then he backed away from me, motioning for me to stay put. I obeyed him. He stepped through the open courtyard gates. A moment later, the gates clanged shut and I heard a metal bar being put into place to lock them.

The situation was silly in a way. I could simply leap over the wall. But then I remembered that these little people had fed me. They had shot arrows at me, but only when I had startled them. And they had given me a place to sleep that was protected from the rain.

"I'll have to try to learn their language," I said aloud. "And I'll have to show them I am grateful."

I ached in every muscle from my long, cold swim. It was early afternoon, but I crept back into the temple— my new home. I lay down with my stomach on the cool stone floor. "Living mountain." *Quinbus Flestrin.* I knew two words already. I decided to learn more the next day. But for now I was tired. I fell asleep and dreamed that I was running through the green fields of England with my beloved Mary.

Chapter Three

For many weeks, I stayed in the temple or the courtyard that surrounded it. Twice a day, in the morning and then again in the afternoon, horse-drawn wagons brought food and water in to me. My friend who had first shown me the house visited me with others. They turned out to be teachers. I was more eager to learn their language than a terrier in obedience school! Luckily, I always had a knack for foreign languages. So, before long I was able to speak with the people who had rescued me.

Their country, I learned, was an island called Lilliput, and the people there were called Lilliputians. They didn't know anything about my world. They never dreamed that anyone could grow as large as I was to them. The man who had become my friend was in fact a duke named Reldresal. He was pleased at how fast I learned the Lilliputian language, and he often stopped by my temple-house to chat with me.

One afternoon about three months after I had crawled ashore, Reldresal said, "You must be getting tired of staying within the courtyard. Would you like to get out and walk around a little?"

"Will His Majesty allow that?" I asked. By then I had learned that Lilliput was ruled by an emperor and empress. They were the two people who had come out onto the balcony to watch when I had first been brought into the city.

"I will speak to him," Reldresal said. "We may have to arrange things, but it shouldn't be difficult."

I could feel my tail wanting to wag. I had always been a person of action, and being cooped up here was not my idea of a great time. Anyway, I was curious about Lilliput, and I really wanted to get a good look at the country.

The very next day, Reldresal came to see me wearing a big, wide smile. He had with him a treaty, an agreement, written very large on a sheet of paper that—to him—was the size of a medium rug. To me it was about as big as a handkerchief. "His Majesty agrees that you may move around our land freely," Reldresal told me. "First, however, the emperor says you must sign this agreement."

I could not yet read Lilliputian, so he read it aloud to me. The document said that I agreed not to leave the empire without the emperor's permission. "That's fine with me," I told Reldresal. "I'll not go astray!"

He went on. All the terms of the treaty were reasonable. Two representatives of the emperor would examine my belongings to make sure I wasn't carrying anything dangerous. I had to be careful not to step on anyone. I wasn't supposed to enter any town without giving a warning first. I would help the emperor by carrying messages very fast, if need be. And I was never to help Blefuscu.

"What's Blefuscu?" I asked in some confusion.

Reldresal sighed and shook his head. "Blefuscu is a wicked kingdom on a neighboring island," he said. "The people there have been at war with us for many years. They sink our ships and sometimes send raiding armies to burn our houses. But you don't need to worry about that. Will you sign?"

"Bring on the ink," I said. A man rolled in a small barrel of ink and then opened it. I dipped a paw in it, then carefully placed my print on the treaty as proof that I would obey the agreement. "When do we leave?" I asked.

Reldresal laughed. "My friend, we need a little time to get prepared. I'll call on you bright and early tomorrow morning!"

Sure enough, he did. With him, he brought the Frelock brothers, Clefren and Marsi. They were elderly men who worked for the emperor as accountants. They had come to inspect my belongings. The Frelock brothers did, and they made a list of everything that I owned. They admired my eyeglasses, because their own glass was too thin and full of bubbles to make such helpful devices. They loved a telescope I had, and they took turns looking through both ends of it. They puzzled over a small pistol in my waterproof leather bag, but I thought it best not to tell them what it was for. They admired my medical instruments, because their own metals were not as shiny as my highly polished steel. I had not told anyone that I was a doctor, and they did not understand that I used the scalpels when I did operations on my patients. To them, the instruments were so huge that one of them said, "I imagine you must use these sharp, heavy things in order to cut down trees. I will list them as axes."

Lastly, I opened my small change purse for them. There wasn't much money in it—just five Chinese gold coins, worth about five pounds in English money, and a few silver and copper coins.

I told the brothers that I knew it must cost the emperor a great deal to feed me, so I offered to give him all of these coins. The two men were surprised. Clefren said, "Why, sir, you own more gold than anyone in our country!"

Marsi added, "Even one of these huge gold coins would more than pay for all the food you could eat in a whole year!"

"Well," I said, "I can't think of anything better to spend money on than food! I'll give four of the gold coins to the emperor as a present, and you two can share the fifth one."

Marsi had to sit down. "No, no, no," he muttered. "That's far too great a fortune!"

Clefren took off his hat and fanned his brother. "Too much, too much," he agreed. "All our friends would think we were too rich and grand for them! No, sir, please don't give us that much gold!"

At last they agreed to accept a copper penny. When they left, bowing low and rolling their penny along like a hoop, Reldresal laughed. "You've made them very wealthy men," he said. "Now they can retire and live in comfort for the rest of their lives!" He had been sitting on a small stool. He got up and said, "Well,

Quinbus Flestrin Gulliver, are you ready to go out and
meet our world?"

"I was born ready," I told him, so happy that my
tongue was hanging out. "Let's do it!"

As it turned out, that day was a holiday in Lilliput.
The emperor and his whole court were on a wide green
field, as big as a lawn on an English countryside estate. A
huge tournament and fair had been arranged. Reldresal
led me to the emperor, where he announced my arrival.

Then to me, Reldresal said, "Gulliver, I present to
you His Majesty Golbasto Evlame Gurdilo Shefin Mully
Ully Gue, Emperor of Lilliput, Delight and Terror of the
Universe, Monarch of All Monarchs, Taller Than the
Sons of Men, Whose Feet Press Down to the Center of
the World, and Whose Head Strikes Against the Sun."

"Pleased to meet you, sir," I said, thinking that
the emperor's name was about twice as big as he was.

"We are pleased you have learned our language," the emperor said. He turned to his wife. "Aren't we, my dear?"

"Yes, we are," she said, smiling at me. "And now watch as our knights train for battle."

It was quite a sight. I saw tiny knights on two-and-a-half-inch-tall horses jousting and fencing. One of them was very, very good. A thought came to me, and I asked the emperor if I might show him some special entertainment. He said yes, and I picked up an empty hay wagon. To the Lilliputians, it was a big one, but I held it easily in my mouth. I set it down and asked the knight to make his horse jump up into the wagon. When he did that, I picked up the wagon again, very carefully, and held it steady while the knight made his horse step high.

Everyone laughed and clapped to see the horse prance around high up in the air! I wagged my tail and grinned, though I kept a close watch to make sure that the knight and his horse didn't fall out of the wagon.

The emperor enjoyed the sight. When I took the knight down, the emperor asked if he could be lifted onto the wagon. I picked him up, and he looked around at the view, laughing at the top of his lungs. "You should try this, my dear!" he shouted to his wife. "I feel like a giant!"

"No, thank you," the empress said coldly. I think she believed that what her husband was doing was not quite dignified enough for a ruler.

When the emperor grew tired of the game, I set him back on his throne and put the wagon aside. "Tell me, Quinbus Flestrin," he said, "what is your country like? Is anyone else there as big as you?"

"Oh, sir," I said, "some are even larger."

"I don't believe it!" snapped the empress. "Why, just six of you would eat everything on our island in less than a year. People your size can't possibly exist—not in any great numbers, anyway. I think you're the only one of your kind!"

"No, Your Majesty," I assured her. "I come from a much bigger island than Lilliput. It's called Great Britain, and there everything is large—people, cattle, houses, meals."

"Do you have a king on your island?" asked the emperor.

"Yes, sir," I said. "A very wise king. Sometimes he holds tournaments a lot like this one."

"To choose his government?" the emperor asked.

I wasn't sure what he meant. "Sir?"

The emperor waved his hand. "Look over there, for example," he said. I looked, and I saw that some men had set up a tightrope about a foot off the ground. One of them started to walk across it. He got only a few inches along it when he fell off and bounced into a net. He climbed out, looking upset.

"Poor Mofosco," the empress said. "No place for him again this year."

"What are they doing?" I asked.

"Why, it's as plain as the nose on your face—which is pretty plain!" the emperor replied, laughing. "The men trying to walk on the rope want to be my government ministers for the next year. Prime minister, minister of defense, minister of finance, and so on. The one who can walk back and forth across the rope the most times without falling off of it gets the best job. The one who walks the next-longest distance gets the next-best job, and so on."

"But why?" I asked in confusion.

"Because a government has to be made up of men with a good sense of balance," the emperor said with a surprised glance at me. "I need steady men who can be relied upon, of course. Don't they do it the same way in your Great Britain?"

"Well, no," I told him. "Back home, the king usually chooses his friends to be the members of the government."

"Friends?" the empress asked. "What on earth has that got to do with running a country?"

"Well, it means . . . it makes sure that . . . you see, the king and his people . . . I don't know," I confessed.

"I think *our* ways are best," the empress said. "I suppose the king chooses judges in your country from among his friends, too?"

"Well, he chooses from among people he trusts," I said. I could not help thinking that she was right, though. Many of the judges in England were old, sleepy, and not very smart. But they did have friends in the king's court!

"And is there a test for your judges?" asked the emperor.

"Uh . . . I think they have to know Latin," I said. "That's a language that nobody speaks anymore." Now that I thought of it, that seemed to be a pretty useless skill for a judge to have.

"Well," the emperor said, "we feel that a good judge should be a humble man, so we make those who want to be judges creep under a stick. Whoever creeps lowest is the humblest, so he gets the job."

"Provided," said the empress, "that he can leap high, too. After all, a judge needs high ideals."

"Creeping and leaping," I said. Well, maybe English judges weren't so bad, after all! "Got it. If you want to be a judge, you creep and you leap."

"So much better than knowing a language no one ever speaks," the emperor said with a smile.

"Ahh . . . right," I said. "Let me ask you one more thing. How do you choose your generals and admirals? In England, we promote men who fight well in battles. I suppose you have a different way?"

"Scary faces," the emperor said. "The general of the army can make a face—he sort of screws up his mouth like this." The emperor made a silly-looking face. "Then he presses his finger to flatten his nose out like that—well, I can't do it properly. But he can do things with his face that will make your eyeballs want to run around the side of your head and hide in your ears. Ugh! How terrible he can look! It gives me the shivers just to think of it!"

I thought that was very strange. "Why?" I asked.

"Because a warrior has to be fierce, of course! And you show that you're fierce by frightening people!"

I tried to explain why the English way made more sense. "But, Your Majesty, just think about how a soldier who fights in many battles becomes better at what he does! If he's smart and brave, he will be promoted. In time he can become a general!"

The emperor began to giggle. He looked at his wife and shrugged. "Explain it to him," he said.

"I'm sorry, but your way is just odd," the empress said. "I mean, sending them out onto the battlefield? They could get *killed!* And then where would you be?"

"You'd certainly be without admirals and generals!" the emperor said, still laughing. Then his laughter stopped. He looked serious. "And we need all the ones we can get right now, with this horrible war against Blefuscu going so badly for us."

I didn't feel like arguing anymore. It was a good day, and by the end of it, the emperor had picked out a whole new government for the coming year.

Reldresal went back to my home with me and watched me eat my dinner. I offered to share it with him. "Thank you," he said politely, "but I'm not very hungry."

I didn't realize until later in my adventures how watching a giant eat can take away one's appetite. But I'll tell you about that when the time comes. Just then, I asked Reldresal about the war. "The emperor said it wasn't going so well," I said.

Reldresal looked serious. "It isn't," he said. "We've lost more than a hundred men in battles on our own shores over the past year. Now rumor has it that the Blefuscudians are building a gigantic invasion fleet of several hundred ships. They're going to try to sail right into our main harbor, take over the town, and then battle their way far inland to the capital city. We have to be ready for what may well be some deadly fighting."

"What's the war about?" I asked.

"Eggs," Reldresal told me.

I scratched my left ear with my hind foot. "Excuse

me? I must have heard you wrong. I thought you said the war was being fought over—"

"Eggs," Reldresal repeated. He sighed. "Specifically, over which end of a boiled egg you break when you begin to eat it. We are Little Endians, you see. The cursed Blefuscudians are Big Endians."

"I'm not sure I've got the hang of your language," I said. "Helllooo! Testing, testing, testing. Am I coming through? What in the world are Little Endians and Big Endians?"

Reldresal began to pace back and forth. "Well, Gulliver, the problem started years ago. His Majesty's grandfather, when he was still a boy, began to break a hard-boiled egg at breakfast one morning. He broke the big end of the egg, but he cut his finger on the shell. His father, the emperor, made a proclamation that from then on, all Lilliputians were to break their hard-boiled eggs at the little end."

"I see," I said. "And the Blefuscudians—?"

He snorted. "*They* say that it's evil to break your eggs at the little end. According to them, the gods love only the people who break their eggs at the big end. And they have threatened to enslave or kill anyone who disagrees with them—and that's us, of course."

After a moment, I said, "I suppose that it would be foolish to suggest breaking them in the middle?"

"Shh!" said Reldresal, waving his arms. "You want to be hanged for treason? Well . . . we probably couldn't hang you. Do you want to be done away with in some unpleasant way for being disloyal? Because that's what happens to compromisers!"

I lowered my head. "I'm a stranger here," I said,

"but it seems to me that eggs are kind of a silly thing for people to fight and die about."

Reldresal looked nervously at the temple door, but it was closed. He whispered hoarsely, "So do I. But if the Blefuscudians won't give up, neither can we." After a minute, he asked, "Why do your people fight wars? I assume they have wars. We have had them all through our history, and often for reasons that seem even stranger to me than the eggs."

"We do have wars," I said. "And for very good reasons." But then I thought about it. All the many English wars I remembered were fought over what people believed, or because of greed, or because of chairs. For example, one king would say to another, "So sorry, old chap, but I do very much want to sit in the throne that you're occupying. Let's fight about it, shall we?"

Chairs. Was that any less silly than eggs?

After a while, I said, "You know, Reldresal, I'm beginning to think there may not be any good reasons at all for fighting a war."

"I could come around to that opinion," Reldresal said with a tired smile. "But please keep it to yourself. Just remember that as far as you're concerned, Big Endians are bad, and Little Endians are good."

"And Middlers get hanged as traitors," I said.

That night I had a hard time falling asleep. These people had helped me when they might have killed me. I didn't want them to fight and die in a terrible, senseless war. At least the emperor hadn't asked me to go sailing over to Blefuscu and kill everyone there. I wouldn't do that, of course.

But was there a way to bring peace without bloodshed? Could I think of it?

And if I could, was there any way of carrying out such a plan all by myself?

I was pretty sure that people who could go to war over which end of an egg to break weren't going to sit back and listen to my reasonable plan—whatever it might turn out to be.

And you know something? The more I thought about good old England, sensible old England, reliable old England . . .

Where you got to become a judge by speaking a language no one spoke anymore . . .

Where being the friend of the king meant you qualified for a high government office . . .

Where perfectly sane people fought wars over chairs . . .

Well, I became less certain that any plan I, an Englishman, could come up with would be very reasonable to begin with.

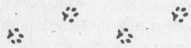

Gulliver has a real challenge on his hands. In the meantime, let's go check on Joe, who has a big game on his hands.

Chapter Four

Wishbone was in the backseat of Ellen's station wagon. His front paws were propped on the back of Wanda's seat. As Ellen drove toward Littleton, some miles north of Oakdale, Wishbone looked left and right, watching the yellow school bus ahead. It was hard for the dog to see, because Wanda was wearing one of her wide-brimmed hats. Every time she turned her head to talk to Ellen, she blocked Wishbone's view.

"What's wrong with Wishbone?" Wanda asked, noticing how every time she turned, Wishbone ducked or stretched.

"I think he knows Joe's on the bus in front of us," Ellen told her. "He wants to keep Joe in sight."

"Well," Wanda said with a sigh, "I just hope the folks at Littleton don't want us to buy Wishbone a ticket!"

Wishbone blinked. "A ticket? I don't need a ticket! After all, I'm one of the guys—and the mascot. Uh . . . Ellen, the players are getting ahead of us again. Pedal to the metal, Ellen? We're not even driving at the speed limit!"

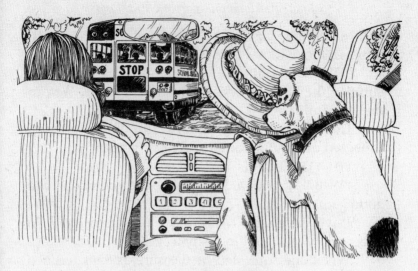

"I hope the boys do well," Ellen said.

"Oh, I'm sure they will," Wanda told her. "I just hope they know what they are in for. The Lancers may be a small team in height, but I happen to know that the Littleton High School basketball team isn't very tall, either, and they've played in the state championships three out of the last five years. There's a lot of talent there."

"I hope the Raiders are up for this game," Ellen said. "Oh, here we are." She parked the car outside the Littleton gym. Then she, Wanda, and Wishbone went inside—after Ellen explained to school security that Wishbone was acting as the Raiders' unofficial mascot.

"Oh, look," Wanda said. "There's Samantha and David over there, with Mr. and Mrs. Barnes. Yoo-hoo!" She waved.

Wishbone had already sniffed out Joe's two best friends. "Cool! Sam Kepler can give the best ear scratches around. And David will always share a snack with a hungry dog! Come on, people, let's move it, move it, move it!"

"Hi," Sam said, as Ellen, Wanda, and Wishbone climbed the bleachers. "Sit right here with us. We can make room!"

David's parents, Nathan and Ruth Barnes, squeezed over, and Wanda and Ellen sat down.

"Hi," David said.

"Well," Wanda said to David, "are you ready for a good game?"

David laughed. "I sure am. I promised Joe we'd cheer really loud, so I'm ready to yell!"

Wishbone squirmed in pleasure as Sam reached down to scratch his ears. She could always hit just the right spot!

"Ought to be an exciting game," Nathan Barnes said. "Coach Gonzalez and Coach Allen were two great basketball players in their time. I remember once when they played against each other in college. Now, that was a game! A fifty-one-to-fifty-one tie at halftime. Finally, Gonzalez and his team pulled out a two-point win. Had us all screaming in the seats."

For a little while Wanda, Ellen, and the Barneses chatted about great basketball teams and players. Wishbone enjoyed Sam's scratching—and the piece of a hot dog that David had saved for him. Then somehow the feeling in the gym changed.

Wishbone straightened up, his black nose twitching. "I smell Joe! He's coming through the door there at the end of the gym in five seconds! Four! Three! Two!—"

Joe and the Raiders came running out onto the

basketball court to the loud, happy cheers of the Raiders' parents and supporters.

Wishbone shrugged. "Just as I said—they came out in exactly *four* seconds. You can't fool the nose! Excuse me, everyone, but duty calls!"

He made his way down to the sidelines. He took his position beside Coach Allen as the Raiders and Lancers got ready to begin the game. The tall man looked down, smiled, and patted him on the head. "I hope you're bringing some luck along with you, boy," he said. "I know Eduardo Gonzalez—and I know we're going to need all the luck we can get!"

Wishbone watched as the other team, the Lancers, came out onto the court. They wore blue uniforms trimmed in black—and, sure enough, they were smaller than the Raiders. A lot smaller. Joe was a head taller than the very tallest Lancer. But the Lancers didn't look as if they were worried.

Wishbone tried to send his thoughts out to Joe: *Play your best against these guys, Joe! Remember, talent can come in very small packages!*

As soon as the game got under way, that was obvious. The Lancers were short, all right, but they were fast! On their very first offensive play, the Lancers did a fast break and rocketed the ball down the court. Wishbone's head jerked as he tried to follow the ball. Whoosh! A lateral pass! Whoosh! Another one! Whoosh! A setup, and where did that Number Thirty-two come from? No matter, he had the ball, he spun and shot, and it was good. The Lancers' fans yelled. A few seconds into the game, and their side was already in the lead!

Wishbone settled down, watching the game. He couldn't believe how speedy the Lancers were. They dove right under the defenders' arms, sensed when they had to pass the ball, and always seemed to be in the perfect position for a shot. Of course, none of them even tried a slam-dunk, but they didn't have to. They were aces when it came to one-handed overhead shots, two-handed set shots, and very accurate when they had a free throw.

The numbers on the scoreboard kept changing, and not in the Raiders' favor. The Raiders never once took the lead. It was the Lancers 8–4, then the Lancers 12–6, 16–8, 22–18. Wishbone groaned as Coach Allen shouted advice and made substitutions. An angry Damont Jones came in off the court, grumbling that the other guys weren't giving him any support. And the score just got worse and worse.

The horn blared to end the half. Wishbone jumped out of his seat as the sound blasted into his sensitive ears. The Raiders came plodding over, sweaty and miserable-looking. "Fifty to forty!" moaned Lewis. "Coach, they're making fools of us!"

"Let's talk about it," Coach Allen said, getting to his feet. "In the locker room. Hustle, guys!"

Guys, Wishbone thought. *I'm a guy!* So he slipped along as the Raiders went back to the locker room. It was a jungle of smells back there—soap and sweaty socks and sneakers, disinfectant, and lockers. Wishbone settled down in a corner. *Come on, Coach,* he thought. *This is the time for coaching. What can we tell these guys that might pep them up?*

The Raiders sat on the wooden benches with their

heads down. Coach Allen said, "Catch your breath." After a moment, he said, "Now, then, this morning someone was saying how the Lancers were going to be pushovers, right? Because they're smaller than we are? Well, they are smaller. But their score looks pretty tall to me right now."

Damont said, "They're better than we are, Coach."

"Could be," Coach Allen said. "Could be. And their coach could be better than I am, too. But let's not look at it that way, because if we do, we beat ourselves." He held up one finger. "You know, I sort of thought we were going into this game with a major disadvantage. Can anyone guess what it is?"

Wishbone jumped up. "I know! I know! Call on the dog!"

Joe said, "Overconfidence, sir?"

"Overconfidence," Coach Allen agreed.

Wishbone sat down. "I was going to say that.

Well, actually, I was going to say 'making a mistake about size and talent,' but I suppose 'overconfidence' sums it up."

"Notice what the Lancers have going for them?" Coach Allen asked.

"They're like a watch," Lewis said. When everyone looked at him, he added, "I mean, all the pieces fit together. They're like a well-built machine. They know what to do, each player works smoothly with the other, and they can spot our weaknesses."

"Teamwork," Coach Allen told them. "Ed Gonzalez has always been famous for it. He always used to say, 'Let the team be the star.' Look how far that took him. Now, what do we need, guys?"

"Teamwork," they all mumbled.

"Say it together!" the coach yelled.

"Teamwork!" they shouted in unison.

"You can do it," the coach told them. "Lewis, you and Joe have that one-two coordination when you're really into your fast breaks. Sean, we're going to give you some chances to hit that basket with your famous layup. Damont, you're great at making shots under pressure, but let's see you pass when there's a shot that you know you just can't make. We're a team! If we all win together, then each of us wins himself!"

Wishbone noticed the guys perking up. He nodded in approval. "Way to go! Come on, guys! They play smart, but we can play smarter! Make those shots! We can do it! Ten points is nothing!"

When the game started again, Wishbone could hardly control himself. He kept wanting to race up and down the sidelines to cheer the Raiders on. And now they were playing a basketball game worth cheering about.

Joe and Lewis worked their magic and scored. Then Sean popped three layups, one right after the other. Soon the score was Lancers 60, Raiders 54. Then the Raiders began to hold the Lancers. The other team was finding it harder to break through a strong defense. Wishbone kept thinking about the score and the clock. Both were creeping up. Was there time for the Raiders to triumph?

With seconds remaining, it was the Lancers 62, the Raiders 60. Wishbone was straining at the sidelines, wanting to run out and help Joe. He didn't, though. He knew that Dr. James Naismith, a phys-ed teacher who had invented basketball in the winter of 1891 in the town of Springfield, Massachusetts, had absentmindedly left dogs out of the rules of the game. But that didn't mean Wishbone couldn't cheer his team on!

The Raiders had the ball and charged down the court. Damont looked as if he were going in for a shot. Then he faked everyone out and sent the ball instead to Joe, who leaped and tossed. The ball hit the backboard, hit the rim, hesitated—and then it dropped inside! The game was tied, 62–62!

Wishbone leaped up and down in his excitement. "Way to go, Joe! Way to go! Two more points now! Just two more points!"

Then the Lancers got the ball and tried their fast break again. Joe tried to cover their Number Seven. But in a lightning-quick move, the smaller Lancer ducked past Joe's defense, caught a pass, did a twisting leap, and threw—

Honn-n-nkk! The closing horn! But the ball was still in play!

Wishbone held his breath!

The ball flew toward the goal—and it swished into the net!

The Lancers' fans went wild! Their team had pulled off a 64–62 victory at the very last second! Wishbone sighed. His tail drooped. The Raiders were dragging themselves off the court, looking crushed.

Joe sank onto the bottom bleacher seat. "Sorry, Coach," he mumbled, his face red and his gaze on the floor. "We let you down."

Coach Allen smiled. "No, Joe. There's no disgrace in losing—not if you played your best game. Anyway, we've got one more shot. If we can play as well against the Jefferson Giants as you guys did in the last half of this game, I'll be happy."

Wishbone put his chin on Joe's knee. "Cheer up, Joe. Sometimes size just doesn't matter. Like in a basketball game when your opponent is quick and charged up."

Wishbone thought about *Gulliver's Travels* again. As Dr. Lemuel Gulliver discovered, a war is always big, big trouble—even when the people fighting it are really, really small.

In the quiet backseat of the car on the way home, Wishbone fell asleep and dreamed again that he was Lemuel Gulliver. He was trying desperately to find some way to end the bitter war between Lilliput and Blefuscu.

Chapter Five

For many weeks I had the run of the whole island of Lilliput. I went all over the place. It wasn't hard, since the entire island was only about twelve miles in diameter. I saw many little villages, and some larger towns. Everywhere the people showed great skill at building. They made houses for themselves in only one day, and not flimsy houses, either, but sturdy, comfortable homes for their size.

Of course, everywhere I went, people came running over to see me. The smaller children loved to ride on my back, though I had to be very careful and gentle with them. The people in the farming villages always gave me some gift—a whole roast ox, about the size of a biscuit; or huge yellow wheels of cheese, no larger to me than a checker from a board game. I was far too polite to turn down any of these treats, and I have to say they *were* very tasty. The Lilliputians laughed when they saw me eat, and they laughed even more when I licked my chops afterward.

After each trip, I returned to my home in the

capital city of Mildendo. The emperor always greeted me when I got back. He would ask, "Uh . . . are you sure you don't have any more of those . . . uh . . . gold coins? They come in very handy."

"No, Your Majesty," I always answered. I had noticed that ever since I had given him my first gift, the emperor had started to become more and more stingy. I suppose that's the way with some people. The more they have, the more they want. At the time, though, I thought that the emperor's growing greed was just something funny. It didn't worry me—then.

About six months after I had come ashore, the emperor notified me that something strange had been found. It was round and black, the size of a small ship. The people who had stumbled across it near the seashore thought it might belong to me. The emperor ordered some workmen and horses to bring it to Mildendo. At that time I was on the other side of the island. When the news reached me, however, I hurried home to see what they had discovered.

It was my hat. I was glad enough to see it, though it was weather-beaten and a little ragged. No wonder, because when I had washed ashore, it was November. Now it was the last week of May. My poor hat had been exposed to the weather for six whole months!

When I put the hat on, everyone admired it. "Why is it round?" Duke Reldresal asked.

"I don't really know," I said.

"If ships were round, it would be the size of a small one," said the duke.

"That gives me an idea, my friend," I said. "Want to climb aboard?" I let Reldresal stand on the brim of the hat. He walked around the brim. "How do you like it?" I asked.

From the front of my hat brim, he laughed and said, "Charming! Almost like flying!"

"Stop that! Stop it this instant!" commanded a shrill voice. I stopped and looked around. An angry Lilliputian, wearing the red coat of an admiral, stood there with his fists on his hips.

"Why? What's wrong?" I asked.

From my hat brim, Reldresal said, "You'd better put me down now. This is Admiral Skyresh Bolgolam." He turned to the Admiral. "Admiral Bolgolam, I'm sure you know Gulliver."

As I lowered my head carefully and let Reldresal step off my hat, the admiral said, "I heard what Reldresal said about ships! Well, *I'm* the admiral around here! If it's like a ship, it's mine! Mine! I should have been given the first ride, not some lowly duke!"

"I'm sorry," I said. "I'll be glad to give you a ride—"

The admiral stomped his feet. "No! Not now! You've already spoiled everything! I hate it when people don't treat me right! You just remember, *I'm* the admiral! Anything like a ship is mine! Mine! Do you understand me? Mine!" He turned away and stomped off, leaving me to stare at Reldresal.

"You've made an enemy, I'm afraid," my friend said quietly.

"I didn't mean to," I answered.

But I had. In the following weeks, Admiral Bolgolam began to complain that the Blefuscudians had almost completed their battle fleet. The admiral said I had done nothing at all to help in the war. Then one day the emperor refused to speak to me. Later that same day, Bolgolam was whispering in his ear and pointing at me. He did not look friendly.

That same evening, I talked to my friend Reldresal about their enemy. The next day, with him and a few workmen riding on my hat, we went to the tallest hill on the north side of Lilliput. From there I could actually see the enemy country of Blefuscu, an island a little smaller than ours. It was only half a mile or so away, across a narrow body of water. I explained to the workmen what I wanted them to do. Then they set to work, cutting down a couple of small trees and building a kind of tripod. When they had finished, I balanced my telescope on it and pointed it at Blefuscu.

The telescope could magnify objects to ten times their normal size. With it, I could see that the invasion fleet was indeed almost ready to attack. "I can count fifty large warships," I told Reldresal, peering at the tiny ships at anchor in the harbor on Blefuscu. Most of them were much larger than my hat. "There are many smaller ships, too. Supply ships, I think."

"Are the masts up on the warships?" Reldresal asked anxiously.

I moved the telescope and focused it. "The masts are up and the sails are ready," I told him.

Reldresal shook his head, looking grim. "Then I think we can expect them in two weeks, when the moon is full. The tide will be high then. They'll be able to sail their ships right into our main harbor, on the far side of the island."

"How many ships do we have?" I asked him.

"Only thirty warships," Reldresal said. "Most of them are small ones, each with only two masts."

I looked through the telescope again and studied the enemy ships. An idea was forming in my mind. "Let's get back to town," I said. "I want to see if the emperor can have some things made for me."

I moved at a good trot, my telescope slung around my neck. Reldresal enjoyed the trip, although I think some of the workers suffered a bit from motion sickness. They looked a little green when I let them get off my hat.

Reldresal and I asked to speak to the emperor, and he agreed to see us. Unfortunately, Admiral Bolgolam was there, too.

"Your Majesty," I said, "I have seen the enemy ships. They have fifty mighty vessels, and many more smaller ones. I think they are planning to invade Lilliput in two weeks."

"Let them come!" Admiral Bolgolam roared, making

a horrible face. "We'll sink them all! Why, just one Lilliputian ship is worth twenty of their worthless Blefuscudian craft! We'll show them!"

I winced. The admiral could be very irritating, like a flea that's found the one place where you can't scratch. His high-pitched voice hurt my ears, too. "I don't think the situation has to come to a battle," I said. Trying to think of some way to get on the admiral's good side, if he had one, I added, "We're bound to lose ships and men, and so are they. But what if I can arrange things so we capture all their ships—without firing a single shot?"

"Not a chance!" the admiral yelled, waving his arms. "Sire, tell this overgrown fool to mind his own business. This is a military campaign!"

"Your Majesty," Reldresal said, "I believe you should listen to Gulliver. I've come to know him very well, and you can rely on his good sense."

"Hmm . . ." the emperor said uneasily, "I don't know." His eyes glittered. "Of course, fifty warships would be worth a lot of money. A *lot* of money."

I felt uneasy for some reason. There was the emperor's greed again. "Yes, sire," I said. "But, of course, the real goal here is to put an end to the war, not to make a lot of money."

"A lot of money . . ." the emperor repeated dreamily. Then he coughed. "Well, tell me, Gulliver, exactly what do you ask of us?"

I bowed, stretching my front paws out and ducking my head low. "My request is simple, sire. Have your chain-makers prepare fifty of the heaviest chains they can handle. I will also need fifty anchors—the biggest ones you can make. With these, I will prevent the Blefuscudians from even setting one foot on your shores."

"Nonsense! We can fight!" roared Admiral Bolgolam. "I *insist* we fight! It will be a glorious battle!"

"Fifty ships . . ." murmured the emperor. "A lot of money. Hmm . . ."

The admiral moaned and groaned, but I could tell that the emperor was interested in my idea. What I was asking for was cheap—much cheaper than building a navy. And of course, as he said, fifty ships would bring him a good deal of wealth—not that he needed it.

Anyway, after thinking it over for a long time, the emperor agreed. It would take about a week to get everything ready. Until that happened, I would stay on the hilltop every day, spying on the enemy.

Days passed. On the seventh day, Reldresal rode out to me on his horse. "How are things over the water?" he asked.

I took my eye away from the telescope. "You were right," I told him. "I've seen soldiers marching onto the ships. And the sailors are rolling barrels aboard. Food and water, I suppose. They're getting ready to sail. Are the things I asked for ready?"

Reldresal nodded. "Yes, but . . . well, I wish you could have stayed in Mildendo. Admiral Bolgolam is convinced you are going to turn against us. He's talking wildly about your being a spy and a traitor, and he's really got the emperor worried."

"I don't think that will last much longer," I said confidently. "If my plan goes well, then by tomorrow morning I should be the hero of the day."

"I hope all goes well, then," said Reldresal.

Wagons brought the chains to me that evening. They were very well made, though each one was so small (to me, anyway) that it was like a fine chain made to string a lady's pearls. The anchors at the end were about the size of fishhooks. I had the royal armorers make one more chain, long enough to go around my neck. Then I had them fasten all the other chains to it. They were a little heavy, but I was pretty sure I could support the weight.

Night came, with a half-moon peeking in and out of clouds. When it was fully dark, I said to Reldresal, "Wish me luck!"

Then, with my waterproof pouch around my neck, I hurried down the hill and to the beach. I waded out into the water. The bottom was a gentle drop. I got nearly halfway across the channel before I had to start swimming. The Blefuscudians had no idea they were in any danger. I could see the burning torch lights of the port ahead, and they helped me judge the current, so that I headed directly toward the enemy port.

I was in the middle of the channel and swimming by then. I let myself sink lower and lower in the water. Only my nose, eyes, and ears were showing. Before long, my feet touched the bottom again. The channel was very shallow. But even when the bottom was under all four of my paws again, I crept along low in the water. Before long, I was right in the middle of the Blefuscudian harbor. Enemy ships were all around me.

Then, suddenly, I heard a voice from up ahead yell out, "What is that thing? Some kind of whale?" I had been spotted! Quickly, I stood up, water pouring

off me. I opened the waterproof pouch and took out my pistol, which was full of gunpowder, and took aim. I hadn't put a bullet in the chamber, though. I didn't want to hurt anyone. I fired the pistol, and the noise from the blast made the Blefuscudian sailors yell in terror. They jumped right off their ships and splashed into the harbor!

I waded right in among them and took one of the anchors in my mouth. I slammed it down on the deck of the nearest Blefuscudian ship, and the hooks bit into the wood. Frightened sailors were still jumping overboard, and a troop of soldiers came hurrying up on deck. However, after taking one look at me, they jumped, too!

I hooked another ship, and another, and another. I worked fast. The water was full of swimming sailors, horses, and soldiers. When I could, I ducked my nose beneath them, scooped them up, then dropped them safely on the piers. This was one naval battle in which no one would get hurt, if I could help it!

Only a few ships remained when finally the enemy organized a defense. The troops began to shoot their arrows at me, but I put on my glasses to protect my eyes and ignored them. Most of the arrows stuck harmlessly in my leather jacket, and the few that hit me hurt no more than a pinprick.

Everything was ready! I had placed hooks into every single ship!

I started to pull. The fifty chains were all attached to the heavier chain around my neck. It tightened as I moved forward and tugged, trying to tow all fifty ships behind me. At first, I wasn't sure if my plan would work. My feet scrambled on the sandy bottom of the harbor. It felt as if I were trying to drag the entire island of Blefuscu.

Then the fifty ships began to move. More men—the last, bravest sailors and soldiers—finally jumped overboard. I heard a little *ping* each time a rope holding a ship to the pier broke. Then I was well under way, dragging the whole Blefuscudian navy behind me!

I could hear the people onshore wailing and screaming in fear. The water got deeper, and I started to dog-paddle. The ships bumped and clanked against one another, but I didn't lose a single one. Once I had them all moving, it got a lot easier to pull them along. With that weight behind me, I couldn't fight the current, but that was all right. Now that I had the enemy ships under control, I could land anywhere on Lilliput!

As it happened, I came back to Lilliput several hundred yards south of the point where I had left. I could see a dozen torch lights on the shore. Then I heard a voice cry out, thin in the darkness: "Gulliver! Are you there?"

"I'm here!" I shouted back. "And I have the whole fleet behind me!"

"Are they invading?" my friend Reldresal yelled, his voice sharp with alarm.

"Captured!" I yelled back. "Every warship they have! Where can I bring them in?"

After a moment, the voice yelled, "There's a big river not too far ahead. I'll ride on horseback along the beach, holding a torch. When you see the torch stop, head for that spot! I'll be standing beside the river!"

And that was the plan I followed. The river, as I

expected, was really more of a brook. However, it was wide enough so that I pulled all fifty ships into it. There they would be protected from the ocean waves. Reldresal and a few of his friends worked through the night with me. We used the chains to tie the ships to trees onshore. When the sun came up, all the Lilliputians were tired but happy. We had indeed captured the whole Blefuscudian fleet, without firing a shot—or, I should say, without firing a bullet.

The emperor hurried from the capital city to see what we had done. He arrived about mid-morning, along with hundreds of his followers. "You did it!" he shouted, when he saw the ships safely in Lilliputian waters. "You brought me fifty lovely, expensive warships! Oh, these will make me rich, rich, rich!"

"But what about our battle?" roared Admiral Bolgolam. "How are we supposed to have a battle if the enemy doesn't have any ships?"

"Oh, be quiet," the emperor said. "Gulliver's the hero of the day! Three cheers for Gulliver!"

Admiral Bolgolam glared at me in anger. He was the only one who behaved that way, though. All the other Lilliputians threw their tiny hats in the air and cheered!

The emperor couldn't wait to tour his new ships. I let him ride on my hat and waded out to the biggest of the captured Blefescudian craft, the admiral's flagship.

The emperor dashed all around the deck. "This is wonderful!" he shouted. "These catapults must be worth fifty gold pieces each! And the ship itself is brand-new! I could get twenty, even thirty thousand gold pieces for it!"

By then the Lilliputians had brought boats. The emperor's sailors climbed aboard them and rowed over to the captured ships. They talked excitedly about how strong and seaworthy the Blefuscudian vessels were. Best of all, every ship was full of food and weapons. I had not only disarmed the enemy, but I had captured some fine meals for myself, as well!

Admiral Bolgolam was the only one who remained unhappy. "This shouldn't count as a victory!" he kept yelling to anyone who would listen. "Gulliver didn't kill a single enemy sailor! And I'm the admiral around here! He kept me from winning a great victory on purpose! He dislikes me! He wouldn't even let me ride on his hat!"

Hardly anyone listened to him, though—or so I thought at the time. Late that afternoon, through the telescope, I saw a small ship leave the harbor at Blefuscu. It sailed across the channel, a blue flag flying from its mast. Reldresal told me that it meant the same thing as an English white flag. The Blefuscudians wished to talk.

Well, what can I say? It was a complete victory. The Blefuscudian king agreed to sign a peace treaty and pay damages to Lilliput for the earlier raids his sailors had made against us. He promised never to start a war against Lilliput again. This war was over without a shot being fired in anger—except for the few arrows that had hurt me no worse than a pesky flea or two.

The emperor's sailors sailed his fifty new ships around to the other side of Lilliput. I returned to Mildendo in triumph, and a huge banquet was given in my honor the next day. I mean *all* day. From sunup to sundown. The Lilliputians served me so many roasts, hams, turkeys, geese, cheeses, and meat pies that I didn't think I'd ever be hungry again—or at least not until the next morning.

There were speeches, speeches, and still more speeches from everyone. The longest one was made by the emperor himself. He reminded me that the day before had been a fine day for a victory. It was, he said, a special date. Exactly nine months earlier, I had washed up on the shore.

"You were truly a gift from the sea," the emperor said. He gave me a medal and said I would go down in history as the greatest hero Lilliput had ever known. I probably should have paid more attention then to Admiral Bolgolam, who glared at me the whole time.

That night the Emperor ordered a display of fireworks. There were skyrockets that shot even higher than my head before they popped, filling the air with glowing red, green, blue, and golden sparks. I was sleepy by then, because I had been up all night before. I politely excused myself from the festivities and went to my house to sleep. Even as I dozed off, I could hear the pop-pop-pop of more fireworks as the Lilliputians celebrated their victory.

I probably slept for about an hour. Suddenly, shouts of "Help! Fire! Fire!" woke me up. I jumped up, rushed outside, and leaped up to put my front paws on the wall around my courtyard. From there I saw a horrible sight.

The tallest tower of the castle was burning! I later learned that a skyrocket had gone off course and had crashed into the tower through a lower window. The whole base of the tower, just where it joined the roof, was on fire! Worst of all, from the upper windows came shrieks and screams. People were trapped in the top of the tower, unable to get down because of the blaze!

I didn't even think. I jumped over the wall, ran to the castle, and leaped up onto the roof. The wooden beams under my paws groaned, and shingles gave way, but the roof held my weight. I ran up the slope until I came to the tower. Even standing on my hind legs, I couldn't reach the trapped people.

I dropped back down and saw the flames shooting through an open window. I suddenly realized that the tower was about the size of a small tree trunk back home in England. I knew very well that water could put out a fire, and I knew exactly where I could get it.

How should I put this? I did a full hind-leg salute. In seconds, the fire hissed out with a boiling, bubbling sound and a cloud of steam! I had saved the day again!

But little did I know that my quick thinking and good aim were about to land me in the worst trouble of my life. As far as the Lilliputians were concerned, I was about to go from "hero" to "zero" in record time.

Chapter Six

Strange days followed the night of the fire, and I didn't know what to make of them. First, workmen tore down the burned tower. When Reldresal came to see me, I asked, "What's wrong? Was the damage so great that the tower was in danger of falling?"

He coughed and said, "Not exactly. The empress ordered that the tower be destroyed. She's upset that you put out the fire by . . . well . . . the way you did."

"But I saved people's lives," I said. "It was the quickest way."

"I know," Reldresal said. He added sadly, "I'm supposed to give you a message from the emperor. You're not to leave your house again until he gives you his permission."

"All right," I said, feeling bad. How could the emperor and empress be angry with me?

Three weeks passed. In all that time, except for the first day, I saw and talked to no one. The Lilliputians would bring my meals to the gate, knock, and leave the loaded wagons standing there.

At last, Reldresal came to visit me again. "I'm so glad to see you," I told him. "It's been lonely for me. I've been on this island for almost ten months now, and I've been away from my home in England for far longer than that."

"I know," he said kindly. "I'm sorry you've been cooped up in here with nothing to do."

"I've had plenty to do," I told him, unable to keep my voice from sounding sad. "I've been remembering my home, and my wife. I've been coming down with a case of homesickness." I sighed. "Any news from the royal court?"

"The peace treaty has been signed," Reldresal said. "The Blefuscudians still refuse to crack their eggs at the proper, little end, but they've promised not to fight a war with us again. We have told them they may crack their eggs at the big end, as long as they keep to themselves."

"Well, the treaty is good news. How's the emperor doing?" I asked.

Reldresal shrugged. "Who knows? He's not talking to me these days. He's talking to hardly anyone except Admiral Bolgolam. I hope he'll soon realize what a mistake he's made by ordering you to be shut in like this. I've arranged for the emperor to speak to you tomorrow. Maybe he'll change his mind then."

The next morning I tried to look my best as I heard trumpets outside the gate. I looked forward to my meeting with the emperor, and I stepped outside my house, into the courtyard, to await his arrival. Servants opened the gate, and then a dozen guards marched through in two lines. Between the lines, eight

Lilliputian soldiers came in. They carried a platform on their shoulders and stopped several feet in front of me. On the platform was a throne, and sitting on the throne was the emperor.

"Your Majesty," I said, bowing low.

"Gulliver," the emperor said coldly, "you have greatly insulted my wife. However, I have thought of a way you can pay for your crime."

"My . . . *crime?*" I asked, hardly able to believe the hurtful word my pointed ears heard. "How can I do that, sire?"

The emperor rubbed his hands together. "The King of Blefuscu probably has great treasures of gold and silver hidden in his palace," he said. "All you have to do is to swim across the channel, tear the palace apart, and bring me back all the gold and silver you can find. And jewels. And anything else that looks expensive."

I closed my eyes. "But, sire, we have signed a peace treaty with the Blefuscudians," I said.

"Nonsense!" the emperor shot back. "You can't trust Big-Endians! Everyone knows that! They'll just wait and then attack us when they think we're not prepared! Why, without his money, the king couldn't supply his military to attack us! And we might even be able to force all the Blefuscudians to break their eggs at the right end! The little end!"

"I am sorry, sire," I told him. "I can't help you."

"I see," the emperor said. "Very well. Guards, take me out of here! And lock the gate behind us!" The soldiers and servants marched out, and then the gate was slammed shut. I shook my head. It would be so easy to leap over the gated wall—but I hoped that Reldresal could talk some sense into the emperor.

Another lonely week went by. Then, late one night, as I lay on my stomach with my head on my paws, I heard the bar that locked the gate being lifted. Then I heard a faint knock at my door. I got up, and opened the door.

Someone wrapped in a dark gray cloak hurried through and closed it. He motioned for me to follow him away from the front door. I lay down again, while he lit a small candle. To my surprise, I saw that the visitor was my friend Reldresal, but in disguise.

"What's going on?" I asked.

"Bad news," Reldresal said. I started to speak. "No, don't talk. Just listen to me. The emperor has turned against you. The empress is angry because she says tearing down the tower ruined the look of the castle. She can never forgive you for what you have done. Worse, Admiral Bolgolam has convinced the emperor that you should have made slaves of the whole country of Blefuscu when you had a chance. He says the peace treaty will only give the citizens of Blefuscu time to gather military strength and attack us again. We'll all have to crack our eggs at the big end, the admiral says, and he blames you."

"But I ended the war," I said, feeling hurt at being so misunderstood.

Reldresal sighed. "I know, I know. But the men who are part of the emperor's inner circle are greedy to grab the riches of Blefuscu. They're talking now about organizing an invasion fleet of our own, using the ships you captured. They want to invade Blefuscu and seize everything the Blefuscudians have. I think the emperor feels the same way."

"No!" I sat up, angry. "I ended the war! Does no one understand that? If we invade Blefuscu, then we'd be no better than the Blefuscudians! I won't hear of it!"

"You won't have anything to say about it," Reldresal said, pulling a sheet of paper from his cloak. "Listen to this proclamation."

As he read, I felt a growing horror. The fur stood up on my neck! Reldresal was reading a court judgment. I had been tried and found guilty of treason—and no one had ever allowed me to defend myself! Reldresal read a list of charges that had been made against me. I had gone to the bathroom without asking permission. I had ruined the castle. I had not killed all the Big-Endians. I had not destroyed the ship that flew the flag of peace. I had not brought all the wealth of Blefuscu to Lilliput.

Listening to these charges, I could only shake my head in wonder. "Of all the small-minded people!" I said. "Do you know what the emperor plans to do to punish me?"

Reldresal dropped the paper on the floor. "He passed a sentence of death," he said in a sad voice. "But I begged him for three days to show you mercy. At last he agreed."

"I'm glad he listened to reason!" I said.

Reldresal turned away from me. "He's sending some soldiers here later tonight," he said in a hoarse voice. "They have orders to shoot arrows into your eyes to blind you. Then you are to become a slave for life." He walked toward the door without looking back at me. "If the soldiers find out I've warned you, they'll kill me, Gulliver. That's all I have to say. Do what you think best."

"You've been a good friend, Reldresal," I told him.

"And I'll never forget you, you—you living mountain," he muttered. Then he slipped out into the night and was gone.

It didn't take me long to pack. I stuffed my belongings into my waterproof pouch, then went outside and leaped over the wall. Just in time, too, because I heard the emperor's guards shout a warning. Then a few of those pesky arrows stuck into my tail. But I ran as fast as I could, far faster than the Lilliputian horses could gallop. I came to the place where all the Blefuscudian ships were anchored.

I roared, "If anyone's aboard, jump off now! This is your only warning!"

Not many people were on the ships—only a few guards. And they fled as I picked up a ship in my mouth and flung it far inland. I threw another, and another. They crashed and splintered to pieces. When they were all broken, I turned and ran northward along the shore. Soon I came to the place where I had swum across the channel to Blefuscu, and I plunged right in. The water was cold, but I didn't mind. I swam right to the empty harbor of Blefuscu and waded ashore, dripping wet.

Then I carefully walked away from the town and lay down in a forest clearing. I spent the night there, cold and lonely.

The next morning, a small group of soldiers came riding up. Behind them was a coach. Out of it stepped a Blefuscudian wearing a royal-looking robe and a crown. I immediately knew that he was the king. "Your Majesty," I said, bowing.

The king looked at me. "I've heard stories about how big you were," he said, "but I never believed them until now. Well, Gulliver, I have had a message about you. A Lilliputian ship brought it an hour ago. It says you are a traitor, and I am to kill you. Otherwise, the Lilliputians will invade Blefuscu."

"They won't invade your island," I said. "I've destroyed all their ships."

"Really?" the king asked. "Well, that's wonderful. In fact, that's just what I wanted to talk to you about. Why stop at just the destruction of the Lilliputians' navy? You could do much more."

I couldn't speak. I just stared at him.

He rubbed his hands together. "We could go far, you and I! Just think of all the possibilities—you could swim across to Lilliput every night and destroy another village. You could tear down their defenses. Break their walls to pieces. You could leave them totally at my mercy!"

"But you promised never to fight them again," I reminded the little man. "You signed a peace treaty."

The king made a shoo-fly gesture. "But that doesn't matter now. Now we have you as our secret weapon! Of course I promised not to fight when we had nothing to fight with! But now you can destroy Lilliput, and then my army will seize control of it! We'll kill those Little-Endians who won't change to Big-Endians. We'll make slaves of the rest. And you can be the governor of Lilliput! We'll rename it Gulliput!

You'll be almost as powerful as a king! What do you say?" he asked slyly.

I didn't say anything. I just got up and hurried away, leaving the king to shout promises behind me, his voice like a bee trapped under a jar. *Great,* I thought, *just great. Here I've brought peace, and no one appreciates it. The emperor of Lilliput doesn't know what peace really is. And the king of Blefuscu is just as bad. The king forgets all of his promises, and the emperor is ruled by greed.*

I walked as far away from the king as I could. I traveled all the way across Blefuscu, ignoring the little people who saw me, screamed, and ran away. Oh, I was careful not to step on anyone, but I didn't want to stop and chat.

I discovered that the north side of Blefuscu was a sandy desert maybe three-quarters of a mile across. I walked through this, hoping no one would follow me. The day was windy. Soon, drifting sands blew, covering even my gigantic footprints. I came to the seashore and sat down, staring out at the distant horizon.

What was to become of me? I wouldn't help the king of Blefuscu in his crazy plan to conquer Lilliput, and I couldn't return to Lilliput because the emperor would try to blind me or kill me. In this tiny land, I also could not live all by myself. I would never be able to find the enormous amounts of food it would take to feed me without being seen. And where could I hide? I was far bigger than a house! Sooner or later, the small folks would discover me, and then the trouble would all start again.

I stretched out on the shore and dozed in the sun. I was already hungry. Would it be my fate to starve to death? I thought maybe I should just paddle out into the ocean and start swimming. Maybe a ship from some faraway country would pick me up. It was a slim chance. I would probably just drown.

I fell asleep as the moon rose. All that night I tossed and turned, scratching my damp hide, hearing the rush of surf, smelling the salty scent of the sea. If only I had some way of getting far, far away from the island! I thought sadly of my wife, Mary, and I was sure I would never see her again. Once or twice I think I actually whimpered.

The night grew cold as the moon began to sink in the west. I woke up shivering just before dawn. I sat up, sand falling off my coat, and shook myself. My mouth was dry, and my empty belly growled.

As the sun rose, I stared out at the ocean again. It had been high tide earlier, but now the tide was out, and the beach was much wider. I could see a large rock, maybe twenty yards across, offshore. Something was on it, something humped and gray. At first I imagined it must be one of those gigantic South Seas turtles, but it didn't move.

Curious, I waded out toward the rock. I had to dog-paddle part of the way. When I got to the mysterious object, I clambered up and stared in disbelief.

Resting upside-down out there on the rock was a weathered gray wooden boat. A wooden boat that would hold *me*. Carved into its worn wood was the word *Antelope,* the name of my sailing ship from England. This must be a lifeboat that had washed up after my ship had sunk!

Ten months before, the ocean had tossed this

boat up on the lonely rock. Because the rock was off the desert side of Blefuscu, no one had spotted the boat. I quickly tried to turn the lifeboat right-side up. When I did, it slid down the side of the rock and into the ocean—

And it floated! I excitedly saw that the supplies were still firmly tied into place under one of the seats. There were six boxes and six small barrels. I knew the barrels held drinking water, and the boxes held food—I hoped it hadn't spoiled. I jumped into the boat, and the swift current began to sweep me out to sea.

To my disappointment, the food *was* all spoiled. But the water was still fresh, and so I drank and drank. Then I explored a little. I found another wooden box nailed to the boat's side. It held some fishing line. Using that and some of the rotten meat from the box I had opened, I started to fish.

Well . . . I learned that you can catch enough fish at sea to stay alive.

Days passed. I drifted to the north, away from the islands of Lilliput and Blefuscu. I tried to use the water wisely, but before long I was down to only half a barrel. Soon, it was clear I was going to be left high and dry, at least as far as drinking water was concerned.

I tried to remember the navigation I had learned. I had managed to rig up a kind of sail for my little boat. I used a mast made from a broken oar that had wedged in the oarlock, and my shirt became the sail. By studying the stars, I estimated that I had gone about two hundred miles from Blefuscu.

Then, on the morning of the ninth day, I saw a sail in the distance. I changed course. Soon it became clear that my new direction would take me right in front of the unknown ship. I could see it was a large ship—large in the way we build them in England, I mean, not in a Lilliputian way. Then, as I got closer, to my great joy I saw the British flag!

A moment later, someone called out to me from the ship. "What boat is that?"

I stood up and waved both paws. "It's an English boat!" I shouted with glee. "With a great big English doctor in it! If your ship is big enough, I'd like to come aboard!"

"Uh . . . I think we can squeeze you in!" the sailor on deck replied. I was not used to normal-sized people anymore. As the sailor reached out to help me up, I roared, "Careful! I don't want to pull you into the ocean with my weight!"

"Why, bless me, I think I can handle your weight," he said, grasping my paw and pulling me aboard with hardly an effort.

The vessel turned out to be an English merchant ship under the command of Mr. John Biddel. I stood blinking aboard Captain Biddel's ship. I dared not move, because I was afraid that I was so large I would turn it over. One of the crew, Peter Williams, stepped forward. "Why, if it isn't the good Dr. Gulliver! How are you, sir, and how do you come to be here?"

I recognized Mr. Williams at once. He had been a patient of mine back at a time when I didn't have very many patients. He quickly told the captain that I was a doctor and a good fellow.

The ship had lost her own doctor in Japan. Captain Biddel and I reached an agreement. He told me we were bound for home. So, for the remainder of the voyage, I was his ship's doctor. By the time we returned to England, on April 13, 1702, I had earned a small salary.

I immediately joined my wife, Mary, and paid off our most important debts. Unfortunately, we were still in need of money. Only two months after my return home, I began to look for another ship to sail on. I was sure that this time good luck would follow me, and that I would return home quite rich and happy.

Well, things don't always work out as they're planned. I was to learn that the hard way.

Size isn't everything. A small person can be a big friend, like Reldresal! Or he can be as small-minded as the emperor or the king. But Joe and his friends have already learned that size can be misleading. Of course, their *next* game isn't going to be played against a small team!

Chapter Seven

Wishbone sat in the driveway and coached as Joe practiced set shots, his specialty. Wishbone turned his head to follow every move of the basketball. He thought Joe was doing a fine job. "Keep your eye on the hoop . . . steady . . . go!"

Joe made the shot, and the ball bounced off the backboard and sailed neatly into the net. "Six in a row," Joe said.

Wishbone jumped up. "Six in a row, so it's time to go! Come on, Joe, it's time for breakfast. You remember breakfast, don't you? It's what you put into a tummy that's become empty overnight."

The door opened, and Ellen looked out. "Joe! What are you doing up so early? It's only six o'clock!"

Joe bit his bottom lip and took another shot. This one swished right into the net. He looked around with a shrug. "My team's got a hard game to play tonight, Mom. If we lose it, we're out of the play-offs. If we win, we're at least tied for first place. I'm really tense."

"Come on in and have some breakfast and tell me about it," Ellen said.

Wishbone ran to the door. "Breakfast! Best way to start the day! Race you, Joe!"

At the table, Joe toyed with his waffles and bacon. Nearby, Wishbone dove into his own breakfast with enthusiasm. Ellen sat at the table, drinking a cup of coffee and looking at her son. "All right, Joe," she said. "What's bothering you so much?"

"We lost last night by two points," Joe said. "And the Lancers are little guys." He shook his head. "They played like a team twice as big as they really are. Mom, tonight we're playing the Jefferson Giants, and they're a tall team. Way taller than us Raiders. It's going to be a hard game."

Ellen smiled. "Don't make it harder than it really is," she said. "If the Lancers played like a team twice their size, the Raiders can do the same thing. Look at it that way."

Wishbone looked up from his empty dish, licking his chops. "That's right, Joe. I've been trying to tell you all along—size isn't everything . . . uh . . . except when it comes to meals. Then my motto always is 'the bigger, the better!' Speaking of which, Ellen, is there any chance for seconds?"

Joe sighed. "You're right, Mom. I mean, I know you're right, but still we've heard that those Jefferson guys are hard to beat. They can outreach us and outrun us. We may get stomped tonight. No one wants to let Coach Allen down. But it's a little scary to think what might happen."

"Scary?" Ellen asked, sounding surprised.

Joe smiled. "Not Halloween-scary. I guess I'm nervous. Last night the smaller team beat us. Tonight we'll find out how it feels to be the smaller guys. But can *we* beat the Giants? We're going to have our work cut out for us tonight."

Wishbone came over and stood on his hind legs, putting his front paws on Joe's knee. "Come on, Joe! Never give up. With the talent on your team, you can play like you're ten feet tall!"

Joe didn't seem convinced. He finished his breakfast. Afterward, he rode his bike over to the basketball camp. Wishbone sped alongside his pal, enjoying the warm Wednesday morning, the bright sun, and the breeze that made his fur ruffle. The morning's practice went well, too. The boys were determined to make up for their earlier loss, although Damont kept saying that the Giants were going to be impossible to beat.

"We'll be lucky to stay within twenty points of

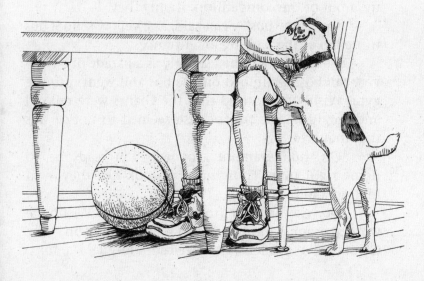

those guys," Damont said. "My cousin has seen some of them play. He's told me they're awesome."

"Then we'll be awesome, too," Lewis returned. "Right?"

Wishbone noticed that the "Right!" the other boys yelled sounded a little uncertain. *Uh-oh,* he thought. *The only thing worse than underestimating your opponent is underestimating yourself! Come on, gang, let's get a little confidence going here!*

That evening, Joe and Wishbone returned to Oakdale College an hour before the scheduled 7:00 tipoff. The rest of the team was there, too, waiting outside the gym. "Hi, guys," Joe said as he got off his bike. "Have they shown up yet?"

"Not yet," Damont said. "We're just waiting to get a look at them."

Wishbone shook his head. There it was again— the feeling that the Raiders were talking themselves right out of the competition. If only they'd—

"Here's the bus!" Sean said, as a yellow school bus turned in at the parking lot entrance.

The Raiders watched silently as a parade of boys— very tall boys—climbed off the bus and went into the gym. Wishbone noticed that the Giants were relaxed and laughing. All anyone else seemed to notice was that they were big.

"Oh, no," Damont groaned. "I'm ready to go home right now. Those guys all look like they're in high school!"

"No," said a voice from behind them. Wishbone whirled around and saw Coach Allen walking up. "The Giants are in the ten-to-twelve camp league, Damont.

They just happen to be a tall team, that's all. We can take them, though, if you'll remember your teamwork and use your heads. Let's go in and suit up."

"What's the use?" Damont asked.

"Come on," Joe said. "All we can do is play our best and hope for a break."

Wishbone sighed. *All this trouble because the other side has a few inches on them. Of course, I can understand that. I'm surrounded all the time by people who are too big! Why couldn't we all be Jack Russell terrier size? That's exactly the right size, in my opinion. Come to think of it, I know just how Gulliver felt on his second voyage. Let's catch up with him and see how that goes.*

Chapter Eight

As Wishbone waited for the game to begin, he once more began to think of himself as Lemuel Gulliver, the poor doctor, off on another long sea voyage. Seeking his fortune, Gulliver set off on June 20, 1702, hoping for better luck this time. . . .

Captain John Nicholas hired me to be the ship's doctor for the *Adventure,* a ship headed around the Cape of Good Hope, at the southern tip of Africa. From there we planned to make a long trading voyage to Surat.

Captain Nicholas understood very well my need for money. He was kind enough to advance half of my pay to me before we set sail on our voyage. I gave it to my wife, Mary.

Again we had a good voyage, at least until we reached the Cape, in Africa. There the poor captain grew ill with a fever. We went ashore and stayed put until the captain was well enough to travel. Unfortunately, the stormy season had arrived by the time the captain recovered.

When we set sail again, at the end of March 1703, we immediately ran into a terrible storm. The wind blew so hard that some of our sails were ripped away from their ropes. It was a fierce gale, a storm with high, howling winds, lightning, and pelting rain.

I'll never forget that awful time! The ship rocked and pitched, and I was sick as a . . . well, sick as someone who was very sick, indeed. The wind howled for five long weeks, and our ship was swept far to the east, into unknown waters. By then we were running very low on fresh water. When at last the storm blew out, we were lost at sea and down to our very last barrel of drinking water.

The captain sailed the ship north, trying to find land. We rationed the water, so each sailor got only one cup a day. My tongue began to hang out from thirst. Finally, on June 16, the lookout on the topmast sighted land. Thanking our lucky stars, we sailed toward it and soon saw it was a large island. Best of all, on the south side a creek bubbled out of the woods and flowed down to the shore. Here was fresh water at last! We were saved!

"Men," said Captain Nicholas, "I'll need a dozen of you to get into the longboat and load our barrels with fresh water. Do I have any volunteers?"

I leaped up and down. "Me! Me!"

The captain laughed and said, "The doctor may go, of course. I take it you are really thirsty, Gulliver?"

"Yes, sir," I said. But the truth was, I really wanted to have solid ground under my paws again!

We rowed ashore, and the other sailors kindly told me they could manage loading the water. They encouraged me to explore, because, as they said, I was a "scientific gentleman," and I might make some interesting discoveries. I trotted about a mile inland. I noticed nothing unusual, except that the grass grew strangely high, towering up to about twenty feet. I guessed it was a species of bamboo, which is only a kind of grass, after all.

I kept hearing rustling sounds off to each side of me, but I could never spot the animals that were making the noise. That was probably just as well. Later I learned they were more than likely insects, large ones. I rested for a little while. Then I headed back to the shore to see if I could help the crew fill the barrels with the fresh water.

Then I heard terrified screams! I ran, but I lost my way. Trotting this way and that, I finally came out on a hill hundreds of yards to the south of the creek. To my horror, I saw the sailors in the longboat, rowing hard and already halfway back to the *Adventure*. They towed a dozen barrels of fresh water behind them. I knew that fresh water in barrels would float in salt water, so that didn't surprise me.

What did surprise and horrify me was that standing in the water, throwing stones at the longboat, was a giant about fifteen feet tall! At that time I did not realize it, but it was actually a boy of only about seven or eight. He probably thought the sailors were some kind of sea creatures. He stood knee-deep in the water and tossed pebbles at them—but he was huge, and the "pebbles" were even bigger than cannon balls! They splashed in

the water and created big waves, but fortunately the giant's aim was very bad. I could see that the longboat was safe, but I didn't know about myself! I turned tail and ran as fast as I could.

In the tall grass I lost my way again. Finally, I stumbled into what I thought was a road, where trees grew on either side. But then I got a close look at those "trees." They were barley plants, but as big as tall pine trees! Their heads of grain were ripe, each one as big as a bushel basket back home.

At that moment, I heard a *swishhh!* and saw the flash of sunlight gleaming on a blade! A giant, twenty times my size, was cutting the grain! The swinging blade whistled just over my ears. It was a good thing they flop downward, or I might have lost the tips!

The twenty-four-foot giant cutting the grain saw me and reached down. I tried to duck out of the way, but he grabbed me with his forefinger and thumb and lifted me high up into the air. He dropped me on the palm of his huge hand and stared at me in amazement. From his pocket he took a red handkerchief the size of a tablecloth and mopped his sweaty face.

"Oh, please don't squish me!" I begged. "I have a wife at home! I'm a doctor! I'm too young to be squished!" I took out of my pocket all the gold coins I had. I offered them to the creature. "Here! Take all of this, please! Just let me go."

The giant stuffed his handkerchief back in his pocket. He licked the tip of a finger and used it to pick up one of the gold coins. He held it close to his nose and squinted at it. Then he shrugged and flicked it away. I could see I wasn't going to buy my way out of trouble. I couldn't help thinking that now I knew exactly how the Lilliputians had felt when I was a giant among them.

Dizzy at that height, I tried to come up with some way to escape that didn't involve growing wings and flying away (because I didn't think I could manage that). Before I could think of any bright ideas, the giant began to talk to me. I dropped to my stomach because his voice was a powerful, rumbling bellow like the roaring of a waterfall. Yet I sensed that he was speaking a real language, not just making sounds, and he did not seem to be angry or threatening.

I yelled to him in English, Latin, and French. He bent over and put one of his big ears within about two yards of me so that he could hear, but he didn't understand a word. I tried speaking Lilliputian, but he didn't know that language, either. The giant farmer finally chuckled and shook his head.

He dropped me into his jacket pocket. I landed on the soft, damp, crumpled-up handkerchief. The giant fumbled with the flap of his pocket and then buttoned it.

Everything went dark!

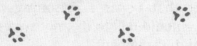

I don't know how much time passed. I could feel the giant walking. It was a bit like being belowdecks in the biggest ship you could imagine. I rocked back and forth, getting thrown this way and that. Hoping I wouldn't get pocket-sick, I held onto the handkerchief to keep from being tossed around. I thought of trying to climb out. But I knew that if I could squirm out of the pocket, it would be easy to lose my grip and fall. And a fall from that great height would surely break my furred neck.

Finally, the giant opened his pocket and reached in carefully. Once again, he took me between his thumb and forefinger, but this time he set me down on top of a gigantic table.

I blinked in the light, and I turned around and around. I was in a farm kitchen, a room larger than any barn I had ever seen. The farmer who had captured me sat at one end of the table. On his right was a woman about his age (he looked about forty), and on the other side was a little girl . . . well, a *big* little girl, if you know what I mean. She looked to be nine years old, but she was a giant, too!

"Hello," I said, bowing. The woman screamed and jumped back from the table. She picked up a huge wooden spoon, and I think she would have smacked me with it and flattened me if the man had not laughed and stopped her. He said something to her, and she said something to him. I believe she thought I was some kind of spider or insect, and he was trying to convince her that I was a reasoning creature. He thought they should talk to me, not swat me. I hoped he would win the argument!

The little girl said something, and the father spoke to her. Then the mother spoke. Then the girl asked a question, and both adults answered her. I noticed that both of the grown-ups used a word that sounded like *Glumdalclitch.*

Guessing this might be her name, I pointed to her and yelled out very loudly, "Glumdalclitch!"

She heard me, and she laughed and clapped her hands. It sounded like two wagons colliding, and the strong breeze from her hand-clapping almost blew me off my feet.

The farmer nodded, as if he were saying "See, I told you he could talk!" He went to a counter, then came back with a bit of bread between his hefty fingers. He offered it to me. It was the size of a whole English loaf. I smiled and then ate the bread, which was coarse. Then I signaled for something to drink. He said something to the woman, and she left the kitchen for a moment. Soon she came back with a thimble, which they filled with milk and placed in front of me. I lapped up the liquid gratefully, thinking that at least I wouldn't starve here!

Before I knew it, I seemed to have become Glum-dalclitch's pet. That afternoon she took me to her room and put me in a cradle that had been made to hold her doll. To me it was like a double-king-sized bed! She sang to me and tried to brush my fur with a toy brush that was about the size of a broom. And she brought me food treats by the ton.

I don't think Glumdalclitch realized how small I was compared to her. When she brought me a piece of cheese, it was as big as I was. When she gave me a piece of chicken, it was enough food for two days. An apple was twice the size of my head. Of course, I had to be polite, so I never turned down a meal.

Glumdalclitch was a chatterbox, and soon I began to learn her language. She talked to me all day, every day. Before a month had passed, I could speak to her pretty well, and I often talked to the farmer, too.

He told me the country I was in was called Brobdingnag, and it seemed that everyone there was a giant! He didn't believe me when I told him about England. He said, "Brobdingnag is the only place there is."

"No," I said. "I've seen many other lands."

"With people like me there?" he asked.

"No—smaller people," I answered.

He shrugged. "Then these other places are of no importance. And we have never heard of any place with small people like you in it. I think you are dreaming, little Gulliver. You are probably some kind of an unnatural being."

I patiently explained that where I came from there were millions of people my size, or just a bit larger. "I have also been to a place where *I* was a giant, and everyone was as small to me as I am to you," I said.

The farmer laughed and said, "Impossible! They would be too small to see!"

Despite his being so annoyingly sure of himself, the farmer was never bad to me. He was a kind man, and his wife treated me nicely. I think, though, that she still thought I was more like a bug. Many times when she first saw me, she would reach for a wooden spoon or a rolled-up piece of parchment paper, as if swatting me was still a possibility.

Of the three family members, Glumdalclitch was my true friend. She called me *Grildrig*, which meant about the same as the Latin *nanunculus,* or the Italian *homunceletino,* or the plain old English "itty-bitty guy." As time passed, I got bored. Being a child's toy wasn't the profession I would have chosen. I began to want to get out of the house. I asked Glumdalclitch if we might leave the farm and go somewhere—maybe to a town.

"Father goes into the village every few weeks to sell our crops at the market," Glumdalclitch said. "I'll ask him if we can go with him next time."

Well, my plan to get out of the house was one of the worst ideas I ever had, as it turned out. I had started something that was bound to lead to trouble. We went to the village market. All around the edge of the market were houses. I was amazed by all of them— larger even than any English castle. The animals, too, were huge—giant chickens, giant horses, giant cows. And if you have never smelled a giant goat, consider yourself lucky. For a couple of hours, Glumdalclitch carried me around in a little box that had holes for windows and air, and I stared in amazement at all the huge things around me.

Someone said, "What's in the box?"

I heard Glumdalclitch reply, "Oh, this is my little pet. I call him Grildrig. He's as smart as could be."

She was so excited that she just had to show me off. She put the box on a flat surface, opened it, and said to me, "Come on out."

I crept out of the box and walked onto the top of a table where they sold food. Seven or eight giants looked down at me, their mouths hanging open.

"Hi, people," I said. "How's the weather up there? Anyone here from out of town? Hey, it's a pleasure to be here. I just flew in from England, and are my arms tired! Anybody here know what a joke is? Are you a live audience or an oil painting?"

The giants began to gasp in astonishment. More

and more of them came over to get a good look at me.
I talked until I started to get hoarse.

"Do something," Glumdalclitch told me. "Show
them some tricks."

"Hum a tune," I told her. When she did, I danced
a little. I sang a few songs she had taught me. I turned
some backflips.

By then the crowd had grown huge. Glumdalclitch's
father came out of a shop and ran over to us to see
what was going on. He told Glumdalclitch that she
had better put me away so I wouldn't get tired. As I
crept back into my box, something crashed onto the
tabletop. I spun around and saw that it was a gold piece
the size of a dinner plate! The giants were tossing money
to Glumdalclitch in appreciation for my performance!
Before we left the market, she had collected twenty-

seven gold pieces. She gave the smallest one, about the size of a saucer, to me. It was so heavy I could hardly lift it!

This gave her father ideas. The next week, he took Glumdalclitch and me farther away, to a bigger town. He hired a boy to go all over town telling everyone that I was the eighth wonder of Brobdingnag. They were invited to come see me in an inn if they paid some money.

All that day the giants paraded to the inn to see me. The first show was before noon, and there were only ten people there. The last one was about nine at night. At that show, about a hundred giants pushed and shoved to see me, talk to me, and watch me dance. I was worn out. I had performed in ten shows!

The farmer was very pleased with the money he made. He began to show me off in other towns. I hated being turned into a public show like that, but I had little say in the matter. Anyway, the farmer had told me he owed money to the local landlord for his farm, and he was afraid of losing his land. He had treated me well, so I agreed to help. I still disliked being shown off like spotted freak.

We spent three months like this, traveling to a different town once a week. Word about me spread, and my shows always brought out huge audiences. The people paid very well to see my act. In fact, the farmer made more than enough money to pay off the mortgage on his farm. I was starting to think it might be time to suggest that I retire from show business.

Then disaster struck.

We were in the biggest town we had visited so far.

It was Lorbrulgrud (which means "Pride of the Universe"), which was the capital of Brobdingnag. It was where the king's palace was. For two days we stayed at the finest inn in town.

Four times a day, I did my performances. Each time the crowds got bigger and bigger. Then, at the very last performance, just as I was finishing my dance, I saw that some giants with swords and helmets were pushing through the audience. One of them said in a booming voice, "In the name of the queen, make way there!"

Everyone grew quiet. I felt the fur on my neck begin to bristle. It wasn't a nice kind of quiet—it was more of an "Uh-oh!" kind of quiet, if you know what I mean. The men seemed to be guards. They came right up to the table where I was standing. The leader bent over and stared at me.

"Uh . . . hi," I said. "The show's free to all our boys in uniform."

"It does talk!" He straightened up and pointed to me. "Who is its owner?" he shouted.

"Hey, hey, hey," I replied "I happen to own myself, thank you! I'm a doctor. I have a license and everything!"

"Shh!" my farmer said. He made frantic shushing gestures. With a hopeful but frightened smile, he said, "Sirs, my daughter owns this little Grildrig."

From inside his uniform, the guard pulled out a leather bag that clinked with the sound of gold. The noise was so loud that it hurt my sensitive ears. The bag was as big as a mattress to me!

"She doesn't own him anymore," the guard said.

"We have orders to buy him for Her Majesty! From now on, he will be part of the queen's collection!"

Poor Glumdalclitch began to cry. She begged the guards not to take me. The farmer tried to talk them out of it, too. After a few minutes, all of the giants—except the guards, Glumdalclitch, and her father—suddenly hurried away.

A giant woman wearing a golden crown came stomping into the inn. Her footsteps were so heavy that the glass in the windows rattled. "What is the meaning of this delay?" she bellowed. I had heard foghorns that sounded softer than her voice. "Someone will suffer for this!"

The head guard knelt down at once. "Your Majesty," he said quickly, bowing his head, "the Grildrig belongs to this child, and she—"

"Yes, yes, I know—she doesn't want to part with it. I know how children are," the woman snapped. "Selfish brats, most of them. Well, who's queen here—her, or me?"

The farmer stammered, "Y-you are, of c-course, Your M-majesty."

She whirled on him and put her hands on her hips. "Are you the girl's father?"

The farmer fell to his knees. "Y-yes, I am, Your M-majesty."

The queen looked long and hard at Glumdalclitch. She put her hand under the girl's chin and made her hold her head up. "Hmm . . . she's not such a bad-looking child. I could stand to have her around, I suppose, if she'll behave herself. Well, what about this? I shall allow the girl to be one of my servants. She can live in the palace and take care of the little creature I am buying. I'll make sure she gets a good education, and you can visit her any time you like. Now, that's far better than you can promise her as just a farmer."

"Y-yes, Your M-majesty," the farmer said, still quaking in his giant boots.

"Is that agreeable?"

"Oh, yes, Your Majesty," said the farmer, "if it's all right with my daughter."

Glumdalclitch sniffled. "I could see my mum and dad whenever I want to?"

"Yes, of course," the queen snapped. "We are not tyrants!"

"And I could keep Grildrig in my room?"

"Yes, but he's mine from now on," the queen said firmly. "If I want to show him off, you have to bring him whenever I tell you to."

"All right," Glumdalclitch said. "Father, I'll do it."

"She'll do it," the farmer said to the queen, as if he were interpreting.

"Good," said the queen. "Because otherwise, I'd have to have the guards chop your heads off." She turned and looked at me. "Are you the little creature that talks?"

"I'm Gulliver," I said. It made me feel annoyed that she hadn't even thought of asking how I felt about this deal. "Now, I happen to be a well-educated man, a doctor—"

"Very amusing," the queen said. "Wrap him up."

Before I knew it, the head guard had scooped me into my box and had slammed it shut. I had been taken out of the frying pan, so to speak, and popped right into the fire!

100

And how about the Raiders? If the Littleton Lancers had been their frying pan—well, I'd say the Jefferson Giants were their fire!

Chapter Nine

"Oh, dear," Wanda said. "It isn't going very well at all, is it?"

Wishbone was sitting in the bleachers between Ellen and Wanda, and just behind the Raiders' coach. Wishbone quickly looked around and then faced Wanda. "Hey, Wanda, the Raiders are behind by only eight points! It isn't *that* bad." He looked back at the court, where the Giants were living up to their name. The tall team had a very good defense.

But, on the other hand, Wishbone thought, the Giants weren't exactly burning up the court, either. Damont had made a couple of good layup shots. So far the Giants had scored only eighteen. . . . *Well, make that twenty,* Wishbone corrected silently as the Giants slam-dunked another basket. The other team's fans cheered wildly.

"I think our team's a little afraid," Ellen yelled over the noise. "They're holding back."

"Well, who can blame them?" Wanda asked. "The Giants' Number Twenty-two is as tall as Coach Allen!"

David and Sam were sitting nearby. "Not really," David said. "He's taller than any of our guys, though."

Sam nodded. "I think the Raiders are just off their game," she said. "They have plenty of time left to catch up. Wait until they hit their stride. I know the Raiders can run rings around some of those Giants."

Wanda suddenly leaped to her feet. She balled her hands into fists and waved them over her head, whooping, "Go! Go! Go! Go, Raiders!"

Wishbone jumped up in excitement. The Raiders had the ball, and Damont was tearing down the court with it. The sound of sneakers pounding and squeaking on the polished floor filled Wishbone's ears as Damont raced toward the basket. Across from Damont, Lewis did some tricky footwork, faked out a defender, and got into the clear. He frantically signaled for the ball— but Damont refused to pass it. He was hemmed in. He tried to get around the defender, and he stepped out of bounds.

"Oh, no!" David groaned. "Damont never wants to pass the ball. But that would have been an easy shot for Lewis."

Sam shook her head. "I think Damont doesn't trust anyone else to make a basket," she said.

Wishbone glanced around. "Excuse me, kids, Ellen, Wanda, but I believe the coaching staff needs my expert advice." He squirmed down to a spot beside Coach Allen, who absentmindedly gave him a couple of pats on the back. Wishbone wagged his tail. "Coach, we need to focus on teamwork for a while. Now, if you ask me, Damont should sit on the bench and let someone else have a chance to play. Did you see—"

"Way to go, Joe!" the coach yelled, jumping to his feet. "Hustle! Hustle! Hustle!"

Wishbone whipped his head around. Joe had intercepted the ball and was in the clear, driving for the Raiders' basket. Well, this was more like it! Wishbone blinked when he heard the sudden roar coming from the crowd. The Raiders' fans screamed encouragement. For a second, it seemed that Joe had a clear shot.

Then the Giants' Number 34, trying to get into position to block, smacked into Joe. The referee blew his whistle as Number 34 fell backward, sitting down hard. Joe took a couple of off-balance steps. Then he fell sprawling, breaking his fall with his hands.

Wishbone was at his friend's side in a moment, with the crowd laughing and cheering at the sight of a dog hurrying onto the court. Wishbone ignored them and looked anxiously at his buddy. "Are you hurt, Joe? How many ears am I holding up?"

The referee came over and leaned down. He put his hand on Joe's shoulder and said, "How about it, Talbot? You okay?"

"I'm fine," Joe said, getting off the floor. Everyone cheered when Joe stood up. He offered his hand to help the opposing player. "You okay?"

The Giants' player nodded as Joe helped pull him to his feet. "I'm really sorry," he said. "Running into you was an accident. I didn't mean to do that."

Wishbone trotted back to the sidelines. "I'm happy to report that Joe Talbot is doing fine! And now he gets two free shots because Number Thirty-four fouled him. He's an expert at them! He once tried to break the world's record! Here's where the Raiders start to catch up!"

Wishbone tensed as he watched Joe take his position. He noticed that Joe stared at the players who toed the lines on either side of him. The Giants towered over Joe's teammates. Wishbone realized that Joe was shaken up—not just by the fall, either.

He tried his first free shot—and missed by inches. The crowd groaned.

"That's okay!" the coach yelled. "Next one, Joe! You've done this shot hundreds of times. Steady, steady, steady! Keep your cool."

But Joe's face was brick-red. Wishbone knew his friend was great at this kind of shot, and he hadn't fallen down that hard. It was clear that the sight of those tall players was making him nervous. Wishbone leaned forward and began to wish for Joe to make the next shot, harder than he'd wished for anything—even steak! Joe got set, made the shot—

The ball hit the backboard, hit the rim, and rolled around to the front. . . . It hesitated. . . .

And then it fell in the wrong direction. The shot was no good.

Wishbone lay down and put a paw over his eyes. "I feel so bad for Joe! He's really trying. The Giants have Joe doubting himself."

Wishbone remembered the trouble that Gulliver landed in when the queen of Brobdingnag bought him as a curiosity. And again, he imagined that he was Gulliver, trying to adjust to his new surroundings and dreaming of freedom. . . .

Chapter Ten

I had been poor all my life. There were times when I had dreamed of living in a palace—but not as part of somebody's toy collection!

That was just what I became in the palace of the king and queen of Brobdingnag. The queen owned all sorts of strange animals—a two-headed turtle, a raven that could talk, and lots of others. And, oh, yes, there was a brown monkey. But to *me,* the monkey was as big as an elephant! Even worse, it wanted to play with me from the moment it saw me.

The queen put me on top of a table. Then the monkey, in a cage hanging nearby, began to chatter. The queen laughed and said, "Let's see what Jocko will do when he sees Grildrig!"

"Uh . . . let's not, if you don't mind, Your Majesty," I said nervously. But she opened the cage, and the monkey leaped out, grabbing at me with its long arms and fingers. I ran away and hid behind a cream pitcher. The monkey chased me around and around it, chattering constantly and flashing its teeth.

"Oh, he wants to play!" the queen squealed with pleasure. "Around and around the little thing goes! Oh, the monkey thinks it's so much fun!"

"Pop goes the Gulliver!" I yelled. The monkey made a sudden, sneaky move toward me and grabbed my jacket.

"Don't!" Glumdalclitch yelled, afraid for my safety. She slapped at the monkey's hand, and it made an angry noise, but at least it let go of me. Glumdalclitch picked me up and put me back inside my little box. "I'm afraid the monkey might hurt him, Your Majesty," she said.

"Child, you may be right," the queen said. "But he did look so funny being chased around like that!"

"I think you hurt Grildrig's feelings," Glumdalclitch said, holding the box out of the monkey's reach.

"Come now," replied the queen. "Nothing so small could possibly have any feelings that matter. But I'll make it up to him. For one thing, I'm sure the royal carpenters can make him a *much* nicer box than that old thing he has now."

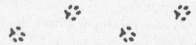

She was right about that. The carpenters carefully measured me. Then they went to work. Within a few days, they had built a most elegant little home for me. To them it was about the size of a lunch box, with a handle on the top so it could be carried easily. It was made of very fine wood, something like cherrywood in color. The inside was padded with a soft, quilted lining. That way, if I were inside the box, I wouldn't be hurt when it was carried around. The carpenters also made me a nice little bed, a chair, a desk, and two chests in which I could place my belongings.

The queen thought it was very funny to have the young ladies of the court sew miniature clothes for me, as if I were a doll. Soon the sewing became a competition. I will say this for the seamstresses—they made a lot of clothes. But I grew very tired of having them insist that I try on five or six outfits a day.

Once the queen had a headache as she watched the younger ladies dress me again and again. She called for her doctor. A huge, heavy giant came in to see what was wrong. I listened as the queen complained of her pounding headache.

The doctor said, "My lady, it is clear that you are suffering from a headache elf. I shall bring you a small rabbit. You must hold it against your head for ten minutes. Then we will let it go, and it will run away with the headache elf inside it."

I could hardly believe my ears. "No!" I yelled at once. "That's just a superstition!"

The doctor turned to me in surprise. "What is this thing?" he asked.

"Oh, that's one of my new toys," the queen said. "He thinks he's just like a real person."

"Madam," I said, "I am a *doctor.*"

The giant doctor said, "That's odd. You dress more like a shepherd."

That embarrassed me. "I can't help what kind of clothes these girls dress me in," I said. "But if you really want to cure a headache, go out to the woods and find some bark from a willow tree. Then boil it. Let the water cool and then drink a glassful of it. That's a very good medicine for—"

The doctor threw back his head and roared with laughter. "The very idea!" he said. "Something this tiny dares to think it could know about a subject as important as medicine!"

"But I *do* know about medicine!" I insisted. "I'm a surgeon, too. I've treated more cases of fever, chills, earache, headache, and toothache than you can shake a stick at . . . or a log, in your case. Which probably is just what you would do, too! Why not? It would help just as much as holding a rabbit to your head!"

The queen smiled. "You know, just listening to his ridiculous speeches makes me feel better. I have a wonderful idea. I'm going to call ten of our kingdom's best doctors together and let Gulliver teach them about his kind of medicine!"

The giant doctor grinned. "That should be very entertaining, Your Majesty," he said.

At first I was excited. I really thought I could do the Brobdingnagians a lot of good. I suspected they were many years behind us English doctors in their knowledge of illness and medicine. It took a week to gather the doctors together. By then my confidence had begun to shrink. When I began my lecture, I could hardly speak loud enough. The sight of all those huge, wrinkled, frowning faces glaring at me made me suspect that they weren't going to listen to me.

And I was right. I began my talk by discussing the circulation of the blood. Before I had spoken for even five minutes, however, the doctors all shook their heads and said, "Preposterous! Rubbish!"

One of them, who seemed to be the oldest, said, "Everyone knows that the purpose of blood is simply to cool a person's brain! And the heart is where ideas come from!"

"Next, the little thing will tell us that bad colds come from tiny little creatures that live in the blood," another one said.

"Gentlemen, colleagues, please," I begged. "I will say this—bad colds can be passed on. You must have noticed that—"

"Well, of *course* they can be passed on!" the queen's doctor said. "That's because Bad Cold Elves call their friends in for visits. When someone gets close enough to a person with Bad Cold Elves inside him or her, then a few of the elves will jump over to the new person!"

"No! No! No!" another doctor yelled. "Bad colds are caused by going out at night when the Bad Cold Star can shine on you!"

All the doctors started quarreling. My tail drooped when I realized none of them were taking me seriously. They thought that just because I was small, I also must be dumb.

But why had the queen wanted me to teach them? Then I realized the reason—she thought it was all a big joke. My feelings didn't matter to her. I looked around. Sure enough, the queen was behind me, in a doorway, laughing her head off. It was clear to me that these huge people really had very small minds. Well, narrow minds, at least. I was never able to pry them open wide enough to force a new idea in.

Glumdalclitch tried to make me feel better. She

didn't like the big dumb doctors anyway, she said. I shook my head. "It isn't that they're *dumb*," I told her. "They're just ignorant. And ignorance can be cured if you try to learn."

None of them wanted to learn from me, though. Gradually, as the weeks passed, the queen got bored with me, so she played with me less and less. That didn't bother me. I was not cut out to be a toy.

The terrible pet monkey often tried to grab me. Glumdalclitch came to the rescue, insisting that the animal not be let out of its cage while I was around. One night I awoke suddenly from a sound sleep when I heard something rattling at my newly built compartment. I panicked and thought it was the monkey, but I quickly lit a candle and opened the door. I was relieved to find that the intruder was just a mouse.

It was large, big as a pony! After watching it for a while, I decided it was harmless. I began to pet it. It came to my door night after night. Very slowly I tamed the mouse. Finally, I managed to train it so I could get on its back and ride around on it as if it were a horse.

After a month or so, I kept the mouse just outside my door one night. The next morning, I rode it out of my quarters when Glumdalclitch brought me my breakfast. She was afraid of it at first, but then she saw how tame it was. She laughed when she saw me ride it around and around a table in the room. "What's his name?" she asked.

I hadn't yet thought of one, but it came to me in a moment. "He's the Wild Mousestang," I told her.

My mouse attracted everyone's attention. For a little while, I had to ride him every day to entertain the queen and her friends. Even the king was interested. He enjoyed the way I rode the Wild Mousestang through an obstacle course. I had him jump over pencils, jewelry boxes, and other items in the room.

The king had hardly noticed me before. After this show, though, he came to visit often. One day perhaps three months after I had been taken to the palace, the king was passing through the queen's sitting room. He noticed me reading a Brobdingnagian book. It was a hard job, because I had to walk back and forth across the page as I read each line.

The king stopped and said, "Can you actually understand what's on those pages?"

I bowed low. "Yes, sire," I told him. "This is a history of your country. The royal tutor taught me your alphabet. Since your kingdom's words are written just as they are pronounced, I have learned to read them very quickly."

"Amazing," the king said. "Read this page aloud for me."

I looked down and started to read. It was all about the Brobdingnagian way of fighting wars, which seemed brutal. The two sides picked up rocks and ran toward each other. Everyone smashed everyone else— even people on their own side, it seemed!

When I finished the page, the king said, "That is extraordinary! Well done! I'll bet your tiny people have no such honorable way of fighting!"

"We fight differently," I told him. "Our armies use guns, not rocks."

"What are guns?" asked the king.

I shouldn't have gone on, but I was irritated by

the way the Brobdingnagians made fun of all my knowledge. I said, "We have something called gun-powder. It's made of charcoal, saltpeter, and sulfur. You mix them together and stuff the mixture into hollow iron tubes and set it on fire. It can send a lead ball whizzing through the air at terrific speed."

"What good is that?" the king asked.

"If the iron tube—that's what we call a gun—and the ball are large enough, they can smash apart castle walls," I said. "And if you shoot enemy soldiers with it, they're almost sure to die. Best of all, you don't have to use any rocks."

"No rocks?" the king said. "No rocks? Then how do you bash people?"

"You don't need to," I said. "The guns do all the bashing for you."

"No, no, no, no," the king said. "Guns seem too dangerous!"

That was when I stopped and thought. Why was I showing off by talking about guns? I didn't even like fighting and killing! In my own way, I was being as small-minded as these giants. "You are right," I said humbly. "I agree. And I would also say that even rocks are too dangerous."

"No. Rocks are traditional," the king said. "Why, when I was young, we had a war. My army bashed three thousand warriors of the other side, plus nearly fifteen hundred of ours! Isn't that wonderful?"

"Wouldn't it be better not to pick up the rocks at all?" I asked.

"Couldn't have a proper war then," the king said firmly. "Got to have rocks. They're traditional."

I gave up. But at least the king showed enough interest to ask me about European history. For many days I told him all I could remember. He especially wanted to know about our wars and our way of government. Finally, though, he told me that he thought I must come from a very lowly culture. "You seem to be such nasty little pests," he explained cheerfully.

"How?" I asked, insulted.

"Well, there's this voting business you talked about," he replied. "You English vote for members of Parliament, and they help to rule you. But what sort of people run for Parliament? The kindest people?"

"Well . . . no," I admitted. "The very kind people usually become charity workers or nurses."

"The smartest people?"

"No," I had to say again. "They become teachers or inventors."

"The most moral people?"

"They usually become preachers," I said.

He went through a long list. Finally, he asked me, "Then what sort of people *do* run for government office?"

"People who are very good at . . . running for office," I said helplessly.

"Well, who'd want to be governed by *them*?" the king asked. "And these wars you brag about—they seem horrible to me!"

"But, sire," I protested, "you brag about bashing people with rocks!"

"Yes, but that's natural," the king said. "But it surely isn't natural to go shooting these guns at people whose religion is different from yours, or who want land you own, or vice versa. I mean, your wars don't even sound like fun!"

And so it went. The king's mind was closed to any new idea. If rocks were good enough for his great-great-grandfather, they were good enough for him. He would lead a band of screaming men into battle, every one of them carrying a boulder. Then he would laugh as he and his soldiers tried to bash everybody in the head. Probably including himself, if he were the only target around.

Some people just resist being civilized.

One good thing did come from my conversations with the king. The queen had kept me shut up in her rooms ever since I had arrived at the palace. I had begun to feel weak and sick for lack of sun and exercise. The king kindly agreed to let me spend some time outside the castle. He had a small part of the lawn walled in and clipped extra short. Then he told Glumdalclitch that she could take me outside every nice day and enjoy the fresh air.

The climate of Brobdingnag was very warm and mild. It was similar to the weather in the Spanish territory of California, in the New World. Just seeing the sun refreshed me. Soon I began to think of trying to escape. These giants with their closed minds were not my kind of people, and I longed to return to a familiar place where I was just the right size.

I realized that would take some doing, though. I began to plot, scheme, and plan, determined to gain my freedom once more.

Chapter Eleven

Months passed. The rainy season came and ended. The queen sometimes showed me off to visitors. More often, though, she forgot about me. Glumdalclitch tried to help ease my loneliness, but she could tell I wasn't happy. She and I often talked about England. Glumdalclitch said she hoped that someday I could return there. Of all the Brobdingnagians, that nine-year-old girl was the only one who believed I really came from a land where others were like me. I knew she would be the one person I would miss—if I ever left the giants' kingdom.

I always had had a good appetite, but the longer I stayed in Brobdingnag, the thinner I became. I believe it was because watching the giants eat made me feel nauseated. Imagine a huge mouth chewing a chicken leg as big as a canoe! Imagine the slurps of a giant drinking from a cup the size of a bathtub! I began to wish that I had been more careful about my table manners while I lived among the Lilliputians!

My loss of appetite did have one good result. I was

able to store food away—dried meats and fruits, plus bits of bread that I wrapped in wax-coated cloth, the same as I did with ship's biscuits. Glumdalclitch talked the royal jeweler into making me some nice little metal cans. Each of them could hold a couple of gallons of liquid. I filled these with water and hid them under my bed. If by some chance I ever found a boat to escape, I would be able to fill it with food and drink to last for at least a month.

More time went by. One night my poor Mouse-stang disappeared. I never found out what happened to him. I hope he got out of the castle without being caught in any traps. As the rainy season passed, Glumdalclitch took me outdoors every single day, because she was alarmed at how pale and thin I continued to get. Nothing helped. The truth was that I was homesick and missed my wife terribly.

More than a year after I had been stranded in Brobdingnag, Glumdalclitch asked me if there was anything that could cheer me up. "Yes," I said slowly. "You know, I was a sailor. Or, at least, I was a doctor who sailed. I would love to see the ocean again, if that's possible."

Glumdalclitch talked that over with the queen. Much to my joy, the girl came back smiling. "The queen says it's time that she and the king pay a visit to Flustrugg," she said. "That's a city right beside the sea. You and I will get to go along, too."

I bowed. "That's wonderful," I said. "Thank you, Glumdalclitch. You're truly a good friend. I'll never forget how much kindness you've shown me."

"Even if you go back to England?" she asked.

I could not keep my tail from wagging, though I felt sad, too. So Glumdalclitch knew exactly why I wanted to see the ocean! "Not even then," I said. "Nothing could ever make me forget you."

For days I planned and schemed. I hoped to steal a boat from the dock at Flustrugg. A small one, of course. I estimated that if I ran back and forth between the boat and my living quarters, it would take ten trips to load up all the food and water I had stored away. Then I would shove off and give all my trust to the sea. British ships sailed everywhere. It would just be a matter of time until one would find me.

The day of our trip came. Glumdalclitch picked up my box very carefully by its handle and carried me onto a royal coach. The trip made sailing on a ship during a storm seem tame. The queen wanted her coach to go fast. The giant horse pulling the coach jolted us over boulders as big as an ordinary house. Even inside my padded home, I had to grip the bed with my mouth to keep from being banged around and bruised. I was lucky the bed was screwed firmly to the wall!

We finally arrived at the city of Flustrugg. As Glumdalclitch carried me into a mansion where the king and queen were staying, I stared out the window of my box. I couldn't see much, but my heart soared at the silver glint of the sea! It was just a matter of time!

That very night, I slipped out of my box. I had talked Glumdalclitch into putting it down onto the floor instead of on a table. All the doors of the mansion were locked, but someone my size could creep through the space underneath the door. Once I made my way outside, I found a warm, bright night with a full moon overhead. My escape was under way.

My sense of smell had always been good. The salty scent of the ocean led me straight to the waterfront . . . and to disappointment. I stood on the beach looking helplessly at two dozen boats pulled up on the shore.

The problem was that I had been in Brobdingnag too long. Giant things had started to look normal to me. The Brobdingnagians did not have ships, only fishing boats and rowboats. But the smallest rowboat was as big as the largest British warship. Foolishly, I had thought one of them would be just the right size for me to use.

I might be able to scramble aboard one. What then? I couldn't row it! I couldn't sail it! I couldn't steer it! I would be stuck.

I thought about making a raft, but there was no time. Anyway, I might be at sea for weeks, and I couldn't trust a flimsy raft to stay afloat. As the tired moon sank in the west, I dragged myself back up the hill to the mansion. I had never felt more sad in my life.

The next day, the same embarrassing public display of me began. In Flustrugg, the local people had not seen me. The queen showed me off for hours. On a balcony, she had me come out onto a tabletop. In the bright sunshine, I sang and danced. The giants tossed grapes at me, which I cut in half with a sword. The queen gave commands, as if I were her lap dog. "Gulliver, run! Gulliver, skip! Good boy! Smart boy!"

I had grown tired of performing like some sideshow act in a circus.

Then the queen said, "Oh, let me show you the funniest thing. Watch what my pet monkey does when he sees the little Grildrig!"

Glumdalclitch put her hand to her mouth in shock. She said, "Oh, no, Your Majesty! Please don't!"

"Quiet, child," the queen said. "It's really the funniest thing." She ordered a servant to get the awful monkey and bring it out on a leash.

I chewed nervously on the hilt of my sword. I was in no mood for that hairy hooligan to paw at me. If it tried, I thought I might stick its fingers with the tip of my sword.

The servant came back in a moment. The second the monkey saw me, it started to screech and try to break away to grab me. "Now hold the leash tightly," the queen ordered the servant. "Put him on the table."

The monkey made a rush at me, but the leash jerked him to a sudden stop. He began to pull and leap, and everyone laughed. I edged toward my box, which stood on the table with its door open.

"Please!" Glumdalclitch said.

Then everything happened at once.

The leash on the monkey's collar gave way with a snap. The monkey jumped right at me. I dashed into the box and slammed and locked the door.

Then I fell against the walls . . . then the ceiling! My home was tumbling end over end!

I heard the queen and the others screaming, but then their voices faded. I found myself lying on the door, which now was the floor. I looked through the window high over the door, and I saw the ground hundreds of feet below.

And I heard the monkey screech.

Then I realized that the monkey was climbing a tall tree. And it was holding my box! Before long, the creature settled on a limb. It began to bang my box against the tree trunk. It was trying to crack my home open like a coconut.

But if it did . . . well, I would have a short but terrifying ride as I fell to the ground!

The monkey saw me staring at it through the window. It bared its teeth and snarled. It tried to stick one of its fingers through a window to pull me out, but the opening was too small.

I backed away as I heard an unearthly screech. The monkey howled in what was either anger or fear. Then the box swayed, and I had the strange feeling that I was rising!

Air rushed past the window, but I didn't seem to be falling. Curiosity made me open the door and peer out. I wished I hadn't.

A small sea eagle had dived down and grabbed the handle of my box away from the monkey! It was soaring away with me, heading for the ocean!

Except it wasn't really soaring. It wasn't flying so much as it was falling very slowly. Probably the varnish the carpenters coated my box with made it hard for the bird to hold in its grasp.

I slammed the door again and locked it. I feared that the eagle would drop me when it realized that it couldn't hold onto me. Then what would happen? Would I be smashed to bits on jagged rocks, or drown in a deep sea?

Whoa! I would soon find out! I was falllliinngggg!

I desperately rolled myself up in the blanket and coverlet on the bed, hoping they would pad me. It seemed I fell for hours, but it couldn't have been more than a few seconds. And then—

Splash!

The box bobbed and rocked back and forth. I had landed in the ocean!

I was sure I was about to drown. Minutes went by.

Then I realized that the box was floating as well as any boat could. My new home now seemed to work like a cork. The Lilliputians may have been the best builders I had ever seen, but the Brobdingnagians really built a nice, strong box! The layers of varnish waterproofed it. I eased over to the door and peeked out the window, which was about two feet above the waves. I could see the island of Brobdingnag, already misty in the distance.

Part of my wish had finally come true. I had escaped from Brobdingnag. But would I ever return to England?

After three long weeks had passed, I was losing hope of ever seeing my homeland again. I was drifting steadily to the south, on a wide and empty ocean. My sturdy box was beginning to show signs of wear and tear. Water was trickling in. Every day I emptied a gallon or so out the window. I was using up my supply of food and fresh water fast.

Then one day I saw a ship! I hoped wildly that it would see me, but I had no such luck. It passed by on the distant horizon. Two days later, I caught sight of another ship, but it, too, failed to spot me.

I knew I must be near the shipping lanes, where lots of sailing vessels passed. How could I signal them? My bed had red silk curtains around it, and I took one down. I pulled some wooden trim off the wall and tore a big square of red silk from the curtains. I tied this to the trim.

The next time I spotted a sail, I pushed everything in my bedroom to one side. The box leaned, then tipped over. Suddenly, the door was on the ceiling! I stood on the edge of the bed and stuck my flag up through the window. I waved that thing for hours.

Then, almost as if in a dream, I heard voices—English voices! Moments later, a thump told me that a ship's boat had come to inspect this strange floating

box. I yelled out, and my cry was answered. Once again I had been rescued.

The ship that picked me up was commanded by Mr. Thomas Wilcocks, who gladly gave me a free ride home. At first he had a hard time believing my fantastic story, though he said it was clear that I had been through an odd adventure. All the English sailors looked tiny to me! I had become used to the giants. Even an ordinary plate seemed no bigger than a button to me. I asked the captain how he could live on a meal as small as the huge turkey he served his officers and me the first evening. And for a long time I could not break myself of the habit of shouting to be heard, instead of talking in a normal tone.

We finally landed back in England. Within two days, I had a joyful reunion with my dear wife, Mary. She told me she never wanted me to go to sea again. The good ship *Adventure* had returned home safely to England many months earlier. The kind Captain Nicholas, sure that I had perished, had given Mary the other half of my salary. He also gave her half of his own share of the items the *Adventure* had brought back from its trading in far-off lands. We were well out of debt.

Best of all, however, I still had the little gold coin that Glumdalclitch had given me. It weighed many pounds, and the money we got for selling it meant that we could live comfortably for years, whether I had any patients or not.

"I'm so glad you're home for good. You'll never have to go on board a ship again," Mary told me.

"No," I agreed. At the time I really thought that was true, but . . . well, my other adventures are another story. Let's just say that at that moment I had seen it all. And let's say that no one had ever been happier to be home and the right size again than your humble servant, Lemuel Gulliver.

Chapter Twelve

Wishbone could hardly stand the suspense. Less than three minutes to go, and the Raiders had the ball—but they were down by six points! The score was Giants 44, Raiders 39. Was there time to save the game? The teams streaked across the court, their shoes squeaking on the floor, their faces red. Both the Raiders and the Giants were tired. Could the Raiders still grab the lead?

Maybe. Since halftime, the Raiders had hit their stride. Wishbone remembered the team had been behind then, 36–14. Now they were playing like a well-oiled machine. But even machines needed time to reach their peak performance.

Lewis came down the court in a fast break. He passed the ball to Joe, who sent it to Damont just in time for a perfectly placed shot! Giants 44, Raiders 41! Wishbone barked, adding his voice to the cheers from the Raiders' fans. "Way to go! Three to tie, and four to win! Let's get some more points, guys!"

Then the Giants had the ball. With so little time

left, it would be easy for them to play until the clock ran out. That meant all they had to do was play very slowly. If the game ended, they would be ahead, and they would win.

Wishbone quickly saw that the Giants did not plan to play out the clock. They headed in for a shot, but again Joe was there to intercept! He sent the ball to Sean, who reversed direction and came in for his smooth layup—and with that basket, the score was Giants 44, Raiders 43.

Wishbone looked up eagerly at Coach Allen. The coach was leaning forward with a big grin on his face. Wishbone put his paw on the coach's knee. "They can do it! If they just continue to work together, I know they can do it!"

Again the Giants had the ball, and this time Damont stole it. He tossed it to Joe. Joe turned, and once more the Giants' Number 34 ran into him.

The ref blew his whistle.

Wishbone felt his heart pounding. "Two more free throws! Oh, Joe, this is our last chance! Remember everything I taught you, and forget about how big the Giants are!"

Joe took his place. He was breathing hard. He clenched his teeth together, held the ball, and hesitated. Then, in one smooth motion, he made the shot.

Wishbone held his breath. The ball sailed through the air, up to the hoop . . .

And went in! Tie score! Wishbone barked in excitement! "One more, Joe! One more! I believe in you! Believe in yourself!"

The Giants were glancing at the clock. Only

seconds were left! What Joe did next would show whether the Giants still had a chance to pull out a win.

Joe got the ball back. He took three deep breaths. He raised the ball and threw it. . . .

Wishbone heard Damont groan in disappointment and say, "Oh, no!"

The ball hit the backboard, then the rim, and seemed to hang there for the longest time!

Wishbone found himself blowing at it!

And then, finally . . . finally . . . the ball fell through the net!

The Giants got the ball back, but they were out of time. The closing horn went *whon-n-nk!* The game was over—the Raiders had won, 45–44!

The Raiders' fans yelled at the victory. Then, as soon as they had fallen silent, Joe led the Raiders as they chanted, "Two, four, six, eight, who do we appreciate? Giants! Giants!"

Joe and the other tired Raiders went to Coach Allen. Lewis was grinning from ear to ear. Right behind them came the Giants' coach. He shook hands with Coach Allen and said, "Great game. Your guys really have it together. Next season they are going to be the team to watch."

"Your players were great, too," Coach Allen said. "I hope they don't feel too low."

The other man laughed. "They don't need to! We've all won, and we've all lost."

Wishbone looked up and saw that Joe was smiling. "It *was* a good game, wasn't it?" he said to Coach Allen. "Even if I did let those Giants psyche me into missing two easy shots."

Damont, surprisingly, slapped Joe on the back. "You weren't so bad, Talbot. You made up for it with those last two! And I have to admit, I messed up, too."

Sean laughed. "But we showed 'em in the end!" he said.

Ellen, Wanda, David, and Sam came down from the bleachers. Ellen said, "Way to play, boys. I really like your spirit."

Wanda nodded. "You would've won by *twenty* points if the other team hadn't been so tall!"

Everyone laughed, and Wanda looked surprised. Joe said, "Miss Gilmore, thinking that all it takes to win a game is height was what was holding us back. I'm just glad we got over it in time."

David nodded in agreement. "And that's what's important—getting the end results!"

Sam reached down to scratch Wishbone's ears. "I think you Raiders cut the Giants down to size," she said. "Anyway, it was an exciting game."

"Well, guys, you played hard and pulled out a great win," Coach Allen said. "Hit the showers, and then let's go downtown. The pizza's on me tonight!"

Wishbone's head snapped up. "Pizza? Pizza? Uh . . . do we all have to take a shower to qualify?"

Coach Allen turned to Ellen and said, "Mrs. Talbot, you and Joe's friends are welcome to come along, too."

Wishbone wagged his tail. "Great, Coach! I want pepperoni!"

Pepper Pete's Pizza Parlor was Oakdale's favorite hangout for whose who liked pizza. In the warm, great-smelling dining room, Wishbone enjoyed a few slices all to himself—and he provided a valuable crust-disposal service for everyone else.

Joe said, "I just wish we'd snapped out of it a little earlier. It's great to win, but I think we should have done better."

"Well, that would've been nice," Sean agreed, battling with a long string of cheese that led from his pizza slice to his mouth. "Still, we did win. We may not be giants, but we played tall in the last half."

Wishbone, gobbling down David's crusts, couldn't help agreeing. "The important thing is that you learned how a team can make every player a little bigger on the court. And that's a lesson you can take with you every time you go into a game!"

Sam leaned over, holding her crust. "Here you go, Wishbone," she said, and Wishbone ran to her.

"Whoa!" Damont said. "Where does that little dog pack it all away?"

Wishbone sniffed. "Little dog, indeed! I may not be as tall as Gulliver among the Lilliputians, Damont, but where pizza is involved"—he took the crusts from Sam and started to chew—"where piffa iff infolfed, I'fe got the affetite of a giant!"

About Jonathan Swift

Jonathan Swift was one of the greatest English satirists. He was born in Dublin, Ireland, in 1667, but both of his parents were English. After he attended Trinity College in Dublin, Swift moved to England. He began to write poems and satires. A satire is a type of humorous writing that points out problems, makes fun of them, and helps people see the need to solve them. While living in England, Swift met such great English writers as John Dryden and Alexander Pope.

In 1714, Swift became a member of the Scriblerus Club, a group of London writers. Alexander Pope was also a member, and so were John Gay and Richard Arbuthnot. The fun-loving writers planned a spoof travel book, to be called *The Travels of Martinus Scriblerus*. Travel books were popular at the time, and many of them exaggerated wildly about strange and exotic foreign places. For a little while, the writers amused one another by making up ridiculous places where their travel book would take place. Swift's friends gradually grew tired of the joke and stopped writing, but Swift kept the plan in mind.

Swift had become a minister in the Anglican church. Late in 1714, he returned to Ireland, where he eventually became the dean of St. Patrick's Cathedral in Dublin. In 1726, he visited his friends in England and let them know that he had finished the spoof travel book at last. This story was the satire that he called *Gulliver's Travels,* and it became Swift's master-piece.

The book was immediately popular when it was published. Over the years, millions of people have read it and have laughed at Jonathan Swift's wonderful fantasy. And they have found themselves agreeing with him when he argues against human foolishness. In Ireland, Jonathan Swift is remembered as a charitable defender of the Irish people. In literature, he is known as a man of great intelligence and great sympathy for the underdog. Swift died in 1745, and he was buried in St. Patrick's Cathedral in Dublin.

About *Gulliver's Travels*

In the 1700s, many people wrote travel books about journeys to strange places. Some of them sound *very* strange to modern readers, because in those days travelers used to exaggerate a lot. They would write about imaginary lands where people had no heads and had faces in the middle of their chests! Other made-up countries had people with only one leg and one huge foot, which they used as a sun shade! Of course, many people realized these tales weren't true.

Among the people who were not fooled was Jonathan Swift. His book *Gulliver's Travels* was published in the year 1726. Its goal was to make fun of such exaggerated travel tales. Jonathan Swift did such a great job that every so often readers thought his story was true. One reader said that he thought *Gulliver's Travels* was a good book, but a few parts of it were a little hard to believe!

In the original book, Gulliver traveled to four strange lands. Two of them were Lilliput and Brobdingnag. The other two were a wonderful floating island where strange scientists ruled, and a country where horses were intelligent, but humans were wild animals.

In all the adventures, Gulliver found societies that just did not understand the English. In time, Gulliver came to realize that that no one—not even the English—knew everything, and that in some ways the English may have been mistaken, too.

Sometimes Jonathan Swift's satire can be harsh

and angry, but more often it makes us laugh at our own human weaknesses and mistakes. That's good, because, as Swift knew, if we can laugh at our faults, we can overcome them. That's a goal worthy of the tallest and smallest among us!

About Brad Strickland
and Barbara Strickland

Brad and Barbara Strickland are a husband-and-wife writing team from Georgia. Brad has written two books in The Adventures of Wishbone series, *Salty Dog* and *Be a Wolf!* Together with his friend Thomas E. Fuller, he has written five WISHBONE Mysteries: *The Treasure of Skeleton Reef, Riddle of the Wayward Books, Drive-In of Doom, The Disappearing Dinosaurs,* and *Disoriented Express.* Brad and Tom also wrote a book for a new Wishbone series, The Early Years story *Jack and the Beanstalk.*

Barbara and Brad have written nine books together, but this is their first in The Adventures of Wishbone series. Brad is an English teacher at Gainesville College, in Georgia. Barbara teaches second grade at Myers Elementary School. The two of them love to travel, and they have lots of hobbies. Brad likes photography and amateur acting. Barbara enjoys sewing and making crafts.

Barbara and Brad have two children, Jonathan and Amy, and a daughter-in-law, Rebecca. Jonathan and Rebecca have a Jack Russell terrier named Falstaff, who gets into about as much mischief as Wishbone! Brad, Barbara, and Amy have a whole houseful of pets, including two dogs, five cats, three ferrets, and an African chameleon named Calypso.

Coming Soon!

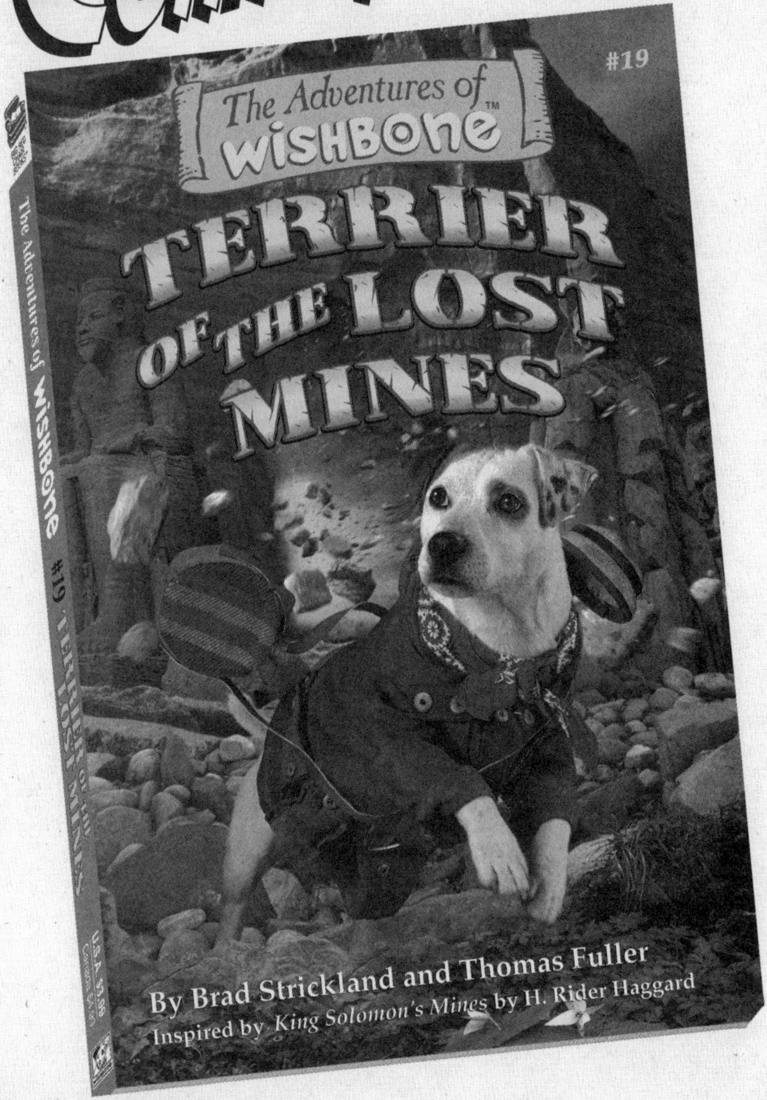
#19
The Adventures of Wishbone™
TERRIER OF THE LOST MINES
By Brad Strickland and Thomas Fuller
Inspired by *King Solomon's Mines* by H. Rider Haggard
The Adventures of Wishbone #19 Terrier of the Lost Mines

Read all the books in the
WISHBONE™ Mysteries series!

The Adventures of WISHBONE

Read all the books in
The Adventures of Wishbone™ series!